# A Guide to Understanding
Eric Voegelin's Political Reality

## Other Books of Interest from St. Augustine's Press

Barry Cooper, *Consciousness and Politics:*
*From Analysis to Meditation in the Late Work of Eric Voegelin*

Francis J. Beckwith, Robert F. George, and Susan McWilliams (editors),
*A Second Look at First Things: A Case for Conservative Politics*

Ellis Sandoz, *Give Me Liberty:*
*Studies in Constitutionalism and Philosophy*

Charles R. Embry and Glenn Hughes (editors), *The Timelessness of Proust:*
*Reflections on In Search of Lost Time*

Ralph C. Hancock, *Calvin and the Foundations of Modern Politics*

Henrik Syse, *Natural Law, Religion, & Rights*

Richard Bishirjian, *The Conservative Rebellion*

Richard Bishirijan, *The Coming Death and Future Resurrection*
*of American Higher Education: 1885–2017*

Thomas Heilke and John von Heyking, *Hunting and Weaving:*
*Empricism and Political Philosophy*

John von Heyking, *Comprehensive Judgment and Absolute Selflessness*

Gerhart Niemeyer, *Between Nothingness and Paradise*

Gerhart Niemeyer, *The Loss and Recovery of Truth*

Roger Scruton, *The Politics of Culture*

Roger Scruton, *An Intelligent Person's Guide to Modern Culture*

Roger Scruton, *On Hunting*

Daniel J. Mahoney, *The Other Solzhenitsyn*

David N. Whitney, *Maladies of Modernity:*
*Scientism and the Deformation of Political Order*

Josef Seifert, *Christian Philosophy and Free Will*

Josef Seifert, *True Love*

Philippe Bénéton, *The Kingdom Suffereth Violence*

Josef Kluetgen, S.J., *Pre-Modern Philosophy Defended*

# A Guide to Understanding
# Eric Voegelin's Political Reality

## Montgomery C. Erfourth

ST. AUGUSTINE'S PRESS
South Bend, Indiana

Manufactured in the United States of America.

1  2  3  4  5  6   25 24 23 22 21 20 19

**Library of Congress Cataloging in Publication Data**
Erfourth, Montgomery C.
A guide to Eric Voegelin's political reality /
by Montgomery C. Erfourth; preface by Ellis Sandoz.
pages cm
Includes bibliographical references and index.
ISBN 978-1-58731-347-9 (paperbound: alk. paper)
1. Voegelin, Eric, 1901–1985. 2. Philosophy, Modern – 20th century.
3. Political science – History – 20th century. 4. History – Philosophy.  I. Title.
B3354.V884E73 2014
320.092 – dc23          2014009623

∞ The paper used in this publication meets the minimum
requirements of the American National Standard for Information Sciences -
Permanence of Paper for Printed Materials, ANSI Z39.48-1984.

St. Augustine's Press
www.staugustine.net

# TABLE OF CONTENTS

# ABBREVIATIONS USED IN TEXT

| | |
|---|---|
| A | Anamnesis |
| AR | Autobiographical Reflections |
| CW | Collected Works, Volume 5 – Modernity Without Restraint |
| EA | Ecumenic Age |
| FER | From Enlightenment to Revolution |
| HG | Hitler and the Germans |
| IR | Collected Works, Volume 14 – Israel and Revelation |
| ISO | In Search of Order |
| MK | The Meditative Origin of the Philosophical Knowledge of Order |
| NSP | The New Science of Politics |
| OH | Collected Works, Volume 1 – Order and History, Israel and Revelation |
| PE | Collected Works, Volume 12 – Published Essays, 1966–1985 |
| SPG | Science, Politics, and Gnosticism (Book 1984) |
| TL | Collected Works, Volume 27 – Theory of Law |

# INTRODUCTION

This is to be a study of political reality and what is required to recognize it. It likely seems absurd to analyze "political reality" given the current state of polarized American politics where the "truth of our situation" is grossly maligned on a daily basis. There is a struggle within society to agree on who we are and what is most important to us, which is played out in the circus of our political representatives' bickering and lack of honesty. America does not seem alone in its struggle to agree on what is "real." There is some agreement among academics and others that throughout the Western world there is a certain level of dissatisfaction within society concerning its representative government's ability to take on what is "real" (Federici, 2002, 18). While the term "real" can have many interpretations, there is a correlation between "real" and "reality." The nexus of these ideas is most likely found in the very meaning and basis of "order" for which the government is *the* representative. Understanding the relationship between order and reality is part of the ancient struggle for society to define human nature and establish a political order that can both honor and impede certain aspects of this nature.

A common "politically conservative" belief is that observing political reality is a matter of common sense and that this reality can be recognized within the totality of Western culture's Christian and Hellenic traditions. This camp would further suggest that the loss of reality is a movement towards "unreality" and that this condition is responsible for the unparalleled human destruction of the twentieth century (Federici, 2002, 16). While those more loosely defined as "liberal" believe that reality is an empirical matter best left to science and that our flirtations with destruction are the result of human systems failing to function properly. In either case, many conservatives and liberals alike agree that there is a looming sense of crisis occurring at the very heart of Western culture that is rooted in how we view the human condition (Federici, 2002, 17).

The West has been very successful and perhaps the most enriched and educated of any collection of people in the history of mankind. This success is often credited to its Judeo-Christian morality, Greek philosophic tradition, Enlightenment ideals, liberal constitutions, rule of law, and powerful economic and military might (Federici, 2002, 15). These ideals and abilities survived two world wars and a third cold one. The West held fast to its traditional beliefs as evidenced by the inherent rejection of and battles against ideologies that crushed individual liberty, ignored the rule of law, and embraced dehumanizing and barbaric practices. The West's defeat and rejection of National Socialism and communism left it free to pursue a reality of its choosing. So why do conservatives and liberals often agree, not on the cause but the sense, that despite its success, there is something wrong within our Western culture?

What political reality needs to be identified and why does it matter? Has science performed some empirical experiments that opened the door to an undiscovered dimension of political reality? For the scientist or layman of today, the surprising answer is "no," but a political reality has indeed been discovered. It was revealed the old-fashioned, and to many the untrustworthy, way of our ancestral past. It was found through the workings of philosophy and the application of reason with its relation to spirit. The man who made this discovery was the eminent twentieth-century political theorist Eric Voegelin. He would tell you that to understand political reality, you have to journey through time, philosophy, social and political order, science, morality, religion, and the ground of being. This journey revealed that the "Western crisis," as he called it, is a sickness in our modern social and political belief system that has led us to a second ordered reality that occludes our eyes from seeing a certain truth in reality. The sickness is the failure to recognize the ground of being as the basis of social and political order.

In a metaphoric sense, Voegelin views Western culture and its highly functioning societies of today as much like a blind Olympic athlete with cancer of the heart and mind. All of the muscle, sinew, lungs, and prowess are present. But the ability to reason and connect with the sacred in our hearts is significantly underdeveloped; the eyes of our soul do not tell us what they see. This leads us to the misuse and squandering of our excellence in the physical realm. It also makes us long for something better we cannot quite identify. Voegelin believed that modernity, despite all its spectacular gifts and progress, has come at a heavy price: the death of the spirit. For Voegelin, the very definition of the modern age is marked by spiritual loss and sickness. Modernity is the spiritually blind Olympian doggedly making its way through history, attaining immense control of the material world but unable to reason, disconnected from the sacred, and sightless to reality. Natural science seems like the best resource available to alleviate this blindness to reality because it has been such a powerful tool in transforming the physical dimensions of life. After all, natural science has been critical in Western culture's ability to move beyond superstition, magic, unreasonable fear of natural phenomenon, and has been a means to understand our place in the physical world. From electricity to engineering, physics, astronomy, medicine, and industry, natural science has revolutionized knowledge.

However, in the quest to understand our material existence, Voegelin felt Western man left behind the exploration of our relationship with the divine (Federici, 2002, 17). Voegelin knew that this might seem like a vestigial appendage to a modern man, but he thought that knowledge of the divine has been both our most ancient and important quest (NSP, 76–77). He believed the Western crisis was related to the divine and would require an exploration of the human soul to understand and resolve it (Federici, 2002, 20). Most natural scientists would relegate this "human" study to religion and that is not inappropriate. Religion is, however, not the only possible means of human study. In fact there is a science older than, and in actuality gave birth to, the natural sciences. It is a science that has been devoted to the exploration of humanity since the time of ancient Greece: philosophy (NSP, 2). Philosophy is perhaps better suited to the task of understanding man than any other means and plays a central role in Eric Voegelin's analysis of the problem of a lost political reality that is so central to the Western crisis (Federici, 2002, 22–23). Religion, like natural science, is an important pursuit, but the skills and methods developed by Plato and Aristotle make philosophy the best and most appropriate tool for the job.

Eric Voegelin dedicated his life's work to defining the "sickness" he saw in Western modernity and developed a new science within the philosophic tradition to adequately expose and address the problem (Federici, 2002, 22–26). His many years of exhaustive research brought him to recognize the relationship between human participation with the divine and the ways in which societies used this knowledge to develop morality, a system of law and order, and ultimately understand reality (A, 172–24). Whatever political apparatus society adopted, it reflected man's relationship with the sacred and found its legitimate authority in the sacred ground of being.

From this perspective, recovering an adequate understanding of reality is a philosophical task of great importance. Voegelin's was a project of demonstrating how to explore, define, and articulate the basis of order, which is the fabric of reality itself. Without a proper understanding of reality, which has a spiritual dignity and guiding hand at its core, the risk becomes ever greater that Western society and politics may continue to deteriorate and ultimately fail to serve its ultimate purpose of sustaining order and attuning society to the "good life" conceived by Aristotle and Plato.

Voegelin recognizes that the sacred has been at the heart of great civilizations and societies for most of man's communal existence. The modern Western urge to revolt against its traditional basis of order in the ground of being, which he identifies as a Gnostic malformation, is the sickness Voegelin demands we cure (Sandoz, 1981, 114). Voegelin is a man living in the desperate tension between two poles. On the one hand, he recognized that the divine ground of being is the basis of all legitimate order, and on other hand that Gnostic thinkers are imperiling society by convincing them to abandon this belief (Sandoz, 1981, 115). For most of his career, Voegelin was the revolutionary front guard against the profane forces of Gnosticism he credits with leading man into murderous ideological mass movements like National Socialism and communism. Eric Voegelin the revolutionary, his science, and his findings are the focal point of this guide. This examination of Eric Voegelin the revolutionary, the political theory he develops, his research, and the sickness of the denial found in the Gnostic rejection of the ground of being will ultimately answer the question: what is political reality?

This guide has a specific organization. It is an exploration of political reality, but it does so through the life and works of Eric Voegelin. To that end, the Western crisis Voegelin recognized and resisted is the backdrop of the entire discussion. Additionally, Voegelin's resistance to the Gnosticism he identified will be a constant theme. Therefore, the first chapter will begin with discussion of the Western crisis, explain Voegelin's quest and life, then outline the Gnosticism he believed rejected reality and the symbols needed to capture reality. The problem of truth and reality in Western civilization requires a lot of exposition and is detailed in Chapter 2 along with an explanation of the *noetic* and *pneumatic* experience and Voegelin's theory of consciousness. Understanding these issues is necessary for a discussion of the new science Voegelin is proposing and how it can be applied, which is the focus in Chapter 3. The conclusion will demonstrate how political reality can be revealed as understood through Voegelin's work, and how to live a life that maintains a connection to transcendental truth and knowledge. Some critical analysis and a summary of his contributions are also included in the conclusion. Each chapter will be broken down further as described below.

Chapter one offers a short biography of Eric Voegelin and a sketch of the Western crisis. Because the times in which he lived and his overall experience are so fundamental to understanding his revolutionary zeal and broad scope of interests, a short but instructive sketch of his life and work is necessary. This will include his life events and discussion of the personal traits and inclinations that make him a unique and distinct figure worthy of study. Because this is a work of and about science, an explanation is provided on Voegelin's views on the seemingly unscientific use of the concept of God and the divine found throughout Voegelin's work. This will help the reader orient with regard to the use of the term. This guide, and Voegelin's own work for that matter, is not an attempt at religious conversion or endorsement for a particular set of religious beliefs. It is merely the exploration of experiences, concepts, and philosophies that concern mostly Western mythical and theological understanding. The third section explains what the term "Gnostic" means according to Voegelin. Exploration of this idea includes Gnostic history, some complications in its use, and how Voegelin's concept of the term evolved over the course of his career. The last section explains Voegelin's use of symbol and language indices. The overall theme is to show the spark, oil, and torch handle that are the metaphoric "flame" of Voegelin's passion to shed light on truth and political reality.

Chapter two begins with an introduction to Voegelin's views of how science, theology, and philosophy were used in the ancient world to reveal truth and the basis of order and how humanity can move away from order by disregarding what the ancients revealed. Voegelin's historical analysis of what leads man to understand human nature through being, origin, and reality are also studied. In section two, one of Voegelin's most important contributions, his theory of consciousness and use of *anamnesis* are detailed. This section further explains how *anamnesis* is a key to unlocking the ancient Greek *noetic* notions of participation, differentiation, experience, and reason that combine in a creative way to know transcendent truth. The third section explains Voegelin's understanding of *noetic* and *pneumatic* experiences. A description of how his thinking evolved on these ideas is necessary and concludes with how he came to incorporate philosophy and theology into a revised science to better research humanity. The fourth section is a description of *noesis'* relationship to political reality and how Voegelin's quest to know truth and reality led him to question the state of political science and modernity's willingness to seek truth. Section five is a brief chapter summary of Chapter two. In a sense, this chapter describes the fanning of the metaphoric "flames" of Voegelinian resistance.

Chapter three begins with a general description of Voegelin's mature political theory. It is best described as what Ellis Sandoz describes as the *Principia Noetica*. In the second section a further discussion of history and revelation is pursued to better fill in important details of this *Principia Noetica*. It can be hard to imagine how to apply Voegelin's highly philosophical work, and the third section of this chapter demonstrates how effective it can be by discussing Voegelin's political analysis of Nazi Germany. The final section will examine Voegelin's critics. Metaphorically, this is Voegelin's passing of the "flame" of passion that is human knowledge.

This guide concludes with a description of Voegelin's contribution to science, his critics, and how the *Principia Noetica* illuminates political reality. This includes a proposal on how to live *La Vida Noetica* and the scientific application of this *noesis*. This guide ends with a few thoughts on Voegelin's overall contribution to human knowledge and citizenship.

# CHAPTER I
# THE FLAME IS LIT

## 1.1 A Man of His Times and His Quest For Truth

### The Crisis of the West That Shaped His Life

Eric Voegelin lived in age of unusually disruptive wars, economic collapse, political strife, and social disruption. While there are few times in human history when a mix of all of these ills has not been present, the twentieth century brought a scale of violence, social dislocation, economic disruption, and suffering to a global level that was both new and horrifying. By the 1950s there was a genuine sense of concern amongst certain academics and social critics about Western culture that on the one hand offered many technical and scientific breakthroughs, while on the other was clearly responsible for the horrors of global wars and societal strife (Federici, 2002, 17). Not everyone agreed on the cause or the nature of the crisis, or that there even was one. For those who did recognize a crisis, a sensible argument enjoined by many liberal-minded intellectuals was that the horrors of the twentieth century were simply the result of dysfunctional social, economic, and political institutions. Conservatives were often more concerned about the growth in state powers and loss of individual rights found in the mass movements of the age. Most liberal and conservative groups universally condemned National Socialism and communism on moral grounds, but all too often only assigned certain causative historical factors but offered no real analysis beyond that. In general, this was often referred to as the "Western crisis" which could likely be resolved through improved policy and better laws (Federici, 2002, 17).

Like many others, Voegelin recognized a "Western crisis" in these modern events of Western history. However, for Voegelin, wars and societal deterioration were the symptoms and not the illness. For Voegelin this crisis was the result of alienation from the spiritual basis of order at the very heart of Western civilization. The Western crisis was one of process and not a singular event, one that continues to unfold in the present (FER, 74). It is a crisis of spirit that will never be remedied through policy or programmatic changes. Voegelin identified a fault line between religious and philosophical transcendentalists who recognized the spiritual crisis of Western civilization on one side, and the liberal and totalitarian immanentist sectarians who rejected this notion on the other (Federici, 2002, 17). This put Voegelin in an awkward position as an academic and was a likely factor in his views not gaining a wider audience. However, this lack of popularity does not diminish the remarkable scope and quality of the scientific, historical, and philosophical output of this remarkable man.

Even with the Western world moving beyond the mass movements of the ideologically driven Nazis and Marxists, the crisis continues. Voegelin believed that the disordering effects of the loss of spirit are continuously at work and reflected in the West's rampant materialism, drug use, social disorders, crime, and general belief that human happiness is achieved through human desire which is not subject to any higher authority. It was to the identification and resolution of this crisis that Eric Voegelin dedicated his life's work.

### A Word on Religion

Some degree of preparation is necessary for the reader of Voegelinian material with regard to his use of terms related to the divine. Voegelin invokes God, the divine, and transcendence throughout his works. For some it can be hard to accept Voegelin as a legitimate scientist, as he frequently seems to bash natural science and promotes God or divinity. This can make people uncomfortable. After all, we have found in natural science an ordinary way to move beyond superstition, magic, unreasonable fear of natural phenomenon, and a means to understand our place in the physical world. The great advancement of human understanding offered by modern-day scientists makes the shaman, mystics, philosophers, clergy, and monks of modernity seem like an unsophisticated vestigial appendage of our older and more ignorant ancestral past. How can Voegelin call on ancient Greeks and St. Paul and think he is promoting science? Isn't he simply promoting Christianity?

It would be easy to form this conclusion, as the use of words like "God," "myth," "eschaton," and "transcendental" can be off-putting in a secular society and somehow outside the sphere of science. However, Voegelin was not actually promoting Judaism or Christianity *per se,* or even a return the gods of ancient Greece. There was a broader undertone to his understanding of the divine that used the symbolism of Christianity because it most clearly represented truth in *his* experience in the *metaxy*. He recognized that man has struggled with the sacred and the profane for the full duration of human existence. Symbols come and go, but in Voegelin's research he concluded that the notion of reality and the articulation of truth are necessary for man to understand himself *through* the divine. It is perhaps best to let Voegelin say it for himself:

> I am indeed attempting to "identify" ... the God who reveals himself, not only in the prophets, in Christ, and in the Apostles, but wherever his reality is experienced as present in the cosmos and in the soul of man. One can no longer use the medieval distinction between the theologian's supernatural revelation and the philosopher's natural reason, when any number of texts will attest the revelatory consciousness of the Greek poets and philosophers; nor can one let revelation begin with the Israelite and Christian experiences, when the mystery of the divine presence in reality is attested as experienced by man, as far back as 20,000 B.C. ... As far as my own vocabulary is concerned, I am very conscious of not relying on the language of doctrine, but I am equally conscious of not going beyond the orbit of Christianity when I prefer the experiential symbol "divine reality" translates the *theotes* and *Colossians 2:9*... Moreover, I am very much aware that my inquiry into the history of experience and symbolization generalizes the Anselmian *fides quarens inellectum* so as to include every *fides*, not only the Christian, in the quest for understanding by reason ... In practice this means that one has to recognize, and make intelligible, the presence of Christ in a Babylonian hymn, or a Taoist speculation, or a Platonic dialogue, just as much as any Gospel. (PE, 293–94)

Voegelin's view of the sacred was expansive and inclusive, not dogmatic. He asks no one to accept Christ as personal savior or to live some typified Christian life. He is suggesting that the notion of God reaching to man in revelation changed how humanity came to know the sacred. The Judeo-Christian teachings are a powerful human tool for order because they offer moral codes that easily translate into laws to govern individuals and political-legal activities. Additionally, prophets like St. Paul preach the wisdom of not seeking perfection of the eschaton in one's mortal life (Sandoz, 2013, 62–63).

When it is paired with the rich understanding found in the exploration of consciousness practiced by mystic Greek philosophy, Christian principles can offer a society the real hope for order and justice as presented by Voegelin (Sandoz, 2013, 85). There is no disputing that Voegelin argues Christianity's symbols are effective. But whatever the divine symbols are for a given society, they only need to be equivalent to those of Christianity, they do not have to be them. The *spoudaios* in his times, through *anamnetic* techniques, and oriented experience in the *metaxy*, who articulates the truth in symbols of the divine ground of being, and recognizes that the horizon of perfection is beyond mortality is all that is required (and obviously a lot is required) (Sandoz, 2013, 62). Allegiance to a dogmatic philosophy or religion is not required, and highly discouraged. This is not the shallow philosophy of a simple ideologue or zealot. It is a spiritual man's recognition of the way to order. This is the time-honored way to political truth and reality.

Voegelin's mystic philosophy was open to the *noetic* science (ancient Greek philosophy) of *experiencing* human life in its rich fullness, not examining it as if he were an outsider (Sandoz, 2013, 81). This is one of Western man's oldest forms of science and can continue to serve us well in its own way to move beyond superstition, magic, unreasonable fear of natural phenomenon, and understanding our place in the physical world in a way natural science cannot. Lastly, Christianity is a fact of Western history and its role in understanding the foundations of Western social morality and governmental institutions cannot be denied. God and the notion of the divine will be used to express Voegelin's insights and theories necessary to understand social and political order throughout this guide. They are never used to advocate a particular belief in the nature of Christ or promote the teachings of the Church.

### *His Quest For Truth*

Eric Voegelin spent his life engaged in an open philosophical search for truth in existence. The responsibility he bore as a political philosopher was to articulate the truth of existence and defend truth from untruth (Sandoz, 2006, 188). Truth and reality wed at a certain level of participation in existence. Truth and reality are often elusive as the possible variations of understanding are endless. A real leap in imagination is required to perceive a more concrete reality. In many ways, untruth is much easier to define. Voegelin spent his life imagining truth through apperception and resisting prevalent ideological distortions (Sandoz, 2006, 188). Diagnosing spiritual causes of these forays away from truth and the historical developments that lead to untruth and resultant loss of reality became his specialty. This put Voegelin at odds with the prevailing thinkers of his day and out of the main-stream of those entrusted with defining social and political truth and reality. It was in this context that Voegelin's identity as the resistor of untruth was forged.

Voegelin recognized early in his career that academics, political actors, and theological institutions were creating deformations in the understanding of truth and reality. Just what he meant by this and how he could demon-strate the veracity of his claims was the opening of a "Pandora's Box" of philosophical, historical, theological, mythical, and political complications (Federici, 2002, 18). His study and conceptions of truth and reality matured over a very long career that spanned seven decades, which makes under-standing his core assertions on the subject something of a journey for the scholar, researcher, or layman alike. For Voegelin this was no mere journey, it was a quest—a quest that, given the age he lived in, took on implications that he came to see as a matter of life and death.

Voegelin's life-long quest to understand the bedrock of existential truth and political reality began from a chain of discoveries. Early in his career, he studied law and the immediate context of the contemporary European political struggle in societies during the 1920s and '30s. He followed this European political morass to the ideas that inspired political struggle throughout history, and from this struggle to the ideas that bonded civiliza-tions. His quest and research expanded in scope, time, and depth over the decades as he unraveled certain mysteries. This chain of inquiry began with the foundational documents that are the agreed-upon structure of states or empires such as constitutions or charters. Voegelin intensively studied these arrangements, how they worked, and how the executive, legislative, and judicial branches functioned or did not. However, he became fascinated by the various ideas buried within the documents that give life and purpose to such political arrangements. From these notions he expanded into the ex-periences of participation in political and social reality where truth becomes a symbolic expression that society then uses as the basis for order and ex-presses in the various charters or constitutions. Voegelin finally arrived at a comparative study of experiences found throughout Western and Eastern civilizations of order and disorder found in the human psyche. Voegelin con-cluded that the best representatives for the ordered psyche were the philoso-phers, sages, and prophets who had done the most to illuminate the ground of being for humanity (Germino, 1978, 111–12). Voegelin came to believe that certain core ideas came to symbolize certain civilizations, and these symbols had to emerge from somewhere. This mysterious "where" was the "somewhere" that Voegelin came to understand as the consciousness of concrete human beings.

It was the deformation of the truth of reality, as found in language and symbol, that sparked a desire in the young Voegelin to resist a pull from a reality that he could sense, but not yet fully define (Federici, 2002, 4). This long quest of discovery was shaped not only by Voegelin's powerful intellect and expansive imagination, but also by the times and events of his life. While the times of any person are instrumental in their own understanding and experience, for a man who studied political theory living in WW I Germany, its chaotic economic and political aftermath, and the rise of Hitler, there was an unusually powerful motivator to seek out truth and resist the deformation of reality and the language used to sustain untruth. To appreciate this man's perspective and motivations, it is necessary to review his life and the trajectory on which his quest ultimately took him.

### His Life and Work

Erich Hermann Wilhelm Voegelin was born in 1901 in Cologne, Germany where his family lived until 1910 when they moved to Vienna (AR, 1989, ix). In 1919, Voegelin was admitted to the Faculty of Law of the University of Vienna. This was his first acquaintance with the classic philosophers, and German idealism as presented in the seminars of Othmar Spann. The works of Max Weber, Alfred Weber, Eduard Meyer, Alfred Spengler and Arnold Toynbee heavily influenced him. The "Stefan George" circle also influenced Voegelin to study the classicists Heinrich Friedemann, Paul Friedlander and Kurt Hildebrandt (AR, 4).

A distorted political atmosphere was increasingly marking post-war Vienna. As Voegelin learned from his interaction with the "Stefan George" circle and the satirist Karl Kraus, one of his primary tasks as a political theorist was to resist the deformation of language by ideological systems (AR, 17). Through the seminars of Hans Kelsen and Ludwig von Mises, he became intimate with a wide circle of sociologists, economists, art historians and lawyers, including Alfred Schütz and Friedrich von Hayek. From these associations, a study group was formed called the *Geistkreis*. Voegelin formed lasting friendships with several members of the group that managed to persist even after many of them were forced to flee Austria during Hitler's rise to power (AR, 18–19).

Voegelin finished his doctorate in political science in 1922 under the supervision of Hans Kelsen and Othmar Spann. He was invited to attend lectures by Gilbert Murray at an Oxford summer school in 1922. In 1924 he was awarded a three-year fellowship from the Rockefeller Foundation that enabled him to spend successive years in New York, at Harvard, Wisconsin, and in Paris. While at Columbia University he studied under Giddings and John Dewey. While at Harvard, it was A. N. Whitehead who opened Voegelin's mind to the idea that he needed to study the origin of ideas in Western culture much more closely. In Wisconsin, Voegelin encountered the practical economics of John R. Commons and labor history from Selig Perlman (AR, 28–33).

It was while in America that Voegelin experienced a sense of revelation at discovering the common-sense philosophy of the English and American traditions, with their foundations so deeply rooted in Classic and Stoic thought. This revelation was further compounded by his study of George Santayana whose open and sensitive, yet philosophic, treatment of the difficulties of the human spirit profoundly impacted the young Voegelin. Santayana accepted neither the dogma nor the neo-Kantian methodologies that so completely governed the philosophies of law and politics that Voegelin had studied in Vienna (AR, 31). In1928 Voegelin published his first book, *Über die Form des Amerikanischen Geistes* (On the Form of the American Mind), where he highlighted his new discoveries (AR, 39). However, despite the wide-ranging studies of Hamilton and Reid, of Santayana, of Jonathan Edwards, and of John R. Commons, he later said that the book never fully conveyed the profound reorientation of his thinking that his encounter with the American political and legal culture had on him. He came to realize that there could be a practical use of Classical and Christian philosophy. Both of these could and had been effectively used in the creation of symbols and language that capture reality in Western societies (AR, 31–33). These seeds germinated and grew into the full flowering of his form of resistance.

In 1926, Voegelin moved to Paris to complete his fellowship. While there, he read the work of Paul Valery that nicely paralleled the *Lucretian* materialism found in Santayana's work, which Voegelin credits as the font of his lasting love for Valery's poetry. In subsequent returns to Paris, Voegelin studied the work of Jean Bodin at the Bibliotheque Nationale. This research, coupled with his reading of Henri Bergson's *Les Deux Sources de la Morale et de la Religion*, was highly influential in laying the groundwork for Voegelin's efforts to relay the foundations of political science in philosophy (AR, 36–37).

Voegelin returned to the University of Vienna in 1928, where he was appointed *Privatdozent* in 1929, and Associate Professor in 1936. He married the silent partner of his later work, Lissy Onken, in 1932 (AR, 51). He became interested in issues concerning race and found a foundation for the work in the philosophical anthropology of Max Scheler. Voegelin's efforts on race and philosophical anthropology resulted in two books published in 1933: *Rasse und Staat* (Race and State) and *Die Rassenidee in der Geistegeschichte von Ray bis Cams* (History of the Race Idea) (AR, 51). During this period Voegelin took lessons in Greek so that he could read the primary sources of Classic philosophy. This enterprise, not unusual for Voegelin, broadened his later study of Plato's works and subsequently enabled him to identify the shortcomings of the philosophical anthropology of Max Scheler (AR, 39). Despite Hitler's rise to power in 1933 and the Austrian civil war of 1934, Voegelin remained convinced that Vienna was safe from any of the Nazi expansionistic plans. His 1936 study, *Der autoritdre Staat* (Authority of the State), was a response to what he felt was National Socialism's deformed concepts of ideologically-constrained politics that were rooted in the intentional malformation of language and symbols (AR, 50).

In Voegelin's estimation, it was the long and steady decline and debasement of the language of political discourse that was the necessary precondition for the rise of National Socialism. The economic and social conditions simply made a debased language and symbolism that much easier to exploit (AR, 47). Voegelin published *Die Politischen Religionen* (Political Religion) in 1938. This was his first major attempt to distinguish the ways in which non-rational formulations of politics could come to dominate social existence. Unfortunately, it was just appearing in print in March as Hitler's troops entered Vienna. The entire edition was confiscated, but later republished by his publisher, Bermann-Fischer, who had relocated to Stockholm (Geoffery Price, 1994). Voegelin described himself as "profoundly shocked" at the destruction of Vienna and the failure of the Western democracies to forestall the annexation of Austria (AR, 42). The failure to prevent the Germans from seizing Central Europe would so obviously lead to a second world war, that Voegelin was absolutely confident England and France would not allow it (AR, 42). Meanwhile, the Nazi occupiers quickly began to investigate Voegelin. Through sheer luck, swift action, and the help of friends he was able to obtain an exit visa before his passport could be confiscated (AR, 43). He raced to the Swiss border before the Gestapo could catch him. Lissy joined him a few days later. Through his contacts in the U.S. he secured a temporary post at Harvard, which enabled them both to immigrate to America (AR, 44).

Once at Harvard, Voegelin busied himself with a job search that would allow for a longer stay in America. He was interested in a position that would allow him freedom from the socialist-leaning émigré scholars in the Northeast, and even turned down a well-paid position at Bennington College (AR, 57). He chose instead a post at the University of Alabama, and shortly thereafter one at Louisiana State University, where he taught American Constitution and Government from 1942 to 1958 (AR, 58). In 1944, he became a naturalized American citizen at which time he Anglicized spelling of his name to Eric Voegelin (Price, 1994).

While at Louisiana State, he undertook the writing of *The History of Political Ideas* between 1939 and 1950. He had set out to trace the origins of political ideas found in dominant societies back to their most basic origins. Voegelin's studies on this subject ran through Thucydides, Plato, Aristotle, Plato, Kierkegaard, and Bacon, to name a few (AR, 78–79). He undertook an examination of the Old Testament and the experiences of several other religious groups as well (AR, 79). In the end, he concluded that it was impossible to trace ideas back in time as he envisaged, as there is no congruency in purely political ideas. Religion, myth, and philosophy shaped society's ideas of order as much or more so than constitutions or political orders, making it impossible to single out purely political strands. He decided in 1950 to abandon *The History of Political Ideas*, but used the massive collection of work assembled over the years as the basis of *The New Science of Politics* and the multi-book project that followed, *Order and History* (AR, 80).

Despite leaving behind a twelve-year effort, Voegelin's years of study had begun to pay off in his ever-increasing understanding of reality, and led to a complete break from the typical epistemological thinking of his peers (AR, 80, 84). In 1952, he released one of his most acclaimed books, *The New Science of Politics* (NSP), which reevaluated the problem of political representation, truth, and the rise of Gnosticism. In this profoundly insightful work he traced the foundation of political symbolism to its roots in the philosophy of the Ancient Greeks and early Christians. Voegelin adopted the term Gnosticism to describe the "sickness" he finds in modernity. For Voegelin, modern Gnostics were individuals, groups, or societies that reject God as the ground of being, assert man's material existence as the only element of reality, and are the progenitors of immanentist programs of world domination. National Socialism, communism, and socialism are simple examples of those political organizations that would be labeled Gnostic. Of course Gnostics would also include those not bent on world domination, but who nevertheless rejected the ground of being and believed that human perfection could usher in a perfect utopian society through systems of science and governmental programs. NSP was a rejection of the Gnostic modernity that Voegelin feared could bring about the destruction of mankind. It remains a concept for which he is best known.

NSP was both a product of his research over the preceding twelve years and a response to the times. By the 1950s fascism was fading away, but the communism of the Soviet Union and China remained living examples of the brutality that a Gnostic order could yield. Voegelin made no effort to write books on the natural evils of the mass-movement systems that he felt these nations engendered. These nations, and the Gnosticism they represented, remained powerful background reminders throughout his career of what man was capable of when uprooted from what Voegelin identified as the ground of being.

He fully expanded his investigation of these Gnostic roots in his next major work *Order and History.* The first three volumes (*Israel and Revelation, The World of the Polis,* and *Plato and Aristotle*) of this five-volume set were released in 1957. In these volumes he reaches back to Isaiah, Jeremiah and Moses, to Homer, Hesiod, the pre-Socratics Greeks, Thucydides, Aeschylus, Aristotle and Plato in order to understand these great thinkers' primary grasp of the foundations of ordered political existence. Voegelin maintained throughout this undertaking that the exploration of our past was not simply the understanding of the past, but to shed light on the contemporary political situation. This situation was, in Voegelin's mind, a struggle in a climate of opinion that obscured the reality of human existence experienced as a tension between mortality and the divine ground of being that the ancients, unlike modernity, understood very well (AR, 80–84). It was during this period that Voegelin began to think of the foundations of political science as more philosophical, and that he would need to assume the role of philosopher to recapture reality. The philosopher does this through the reconstruction of the fundamental categories of existence found in experience, consciousness and reality (AR, 96).

Voegelin was invited to return to Germany in 1958 to head the Institute for Political Science at the University of Munich (AR, 91). Although this position came with an increase in salary, Voegelin relished the idea of returning to Germany to infuse his homeland with the common-sense spirit he had learned in America (AR, 91). New generations of Germans were in need of this injection of fresh ideas and it allowed him to further expand on the foundational work of political philosophy he had achieved during the

'40s and '50s. In 1958, Voegelin also published *Science, Politics, and Gnosticism,* which was the result of his continued research into the ancient origins of gnosis and its connection to the modern form. The book was Voegelin's attempt to highlight the intellectual confusion found in modernity, which he felt was the result of the heavy influence of Gnostic thinkers. Voegelin described "mystic" philosophy as the best relief for the tension caused by this dominant and destructive ideological movement (SPG, 31, 36). He wrote *Anamnesis* in 1966, which could be considered the best synthesis of his political philosophy. He thoroughly explores consciousness, nature, symbols, the ground of being, and reality in this short but densely packed work of remarkable insight and imagination. His task was nothing short of re-establishing the philosophy of history as the manifestation of eternal being in time. This endeavor was meant to communicate the understanding of the truth of human existence under God, which when held as a common belief, brings not only insight and wisdom to a community, but also the most just and stable political and social order. Voegelin's fully matured view of the role of a "mystic philosopher" was to aid society in resisting the pull away from this truth (AR, 96, 100–3).

Voegelin left Germany for good in 1969, when he accepted the position as Henry Salvatori Distinguished Fellow at the Hoover Institution, Stanford, California from 1969 to 1974, and as the Senior Research Fellow from 1974 until his death in 1984 (Sandoz, 1981, 87). He published the fourth volume of *Order and History* (*Ecumenic Age)* in 1974 (Sandoz, 1981, 88). After such a long period between writings for the *Order and History* series, Voegelin's sensitivity to historical data had forced him to revise some of his earlier conclusions about Christianity and the origin of Gnosticism (Geoffery Price, 1994). He also further refined his ideas on symbolism, language, and the inherent tensions between truth and unreality (Geoffery Price, 1994). Voegelin died in Stanford, California, on 19 January 1985, having spent his last days dictating his final meditation *"Quod Deus dicitur"* and refining his thoughts on Gnosticism (Geoffery Price, 1994). The *Order and History* series culminated in *In Search of Order,* which was posthumously published in 1987.

Throughout his career he consistently resisted the temptation to accept convention, go with the crowd, or choose the easy path. From his own experience he knew that a society detached from truth and reality can be horrifically deadly. One of his important discoveries was the rise of Gnosticism, which he felt was a modern deformation of reality and something that was deeply rooted in Western culture and had the potential to destroy it if pursued to its immanental end (Federici, 2002, 183). Voegelin's quest arises in the form of a resistance against the surrounding disorder found in man's existence and the search for historical experiences vital to political and social existential order. He recognized a simple truism about this quest: truth always resists an untruth. Truth and reality are linked as reality is defined by the truth of man's material existence made real through a spiritual ground of being. Those who reject this spiritual nature of man and the human relationship to order were what Voegelin termed "Gnostics." His discovery of the rejection of truth and reality found in modern Gnosticism began in earnest with the publication of NSP and continued for the rest of his career. Voegelin spent a lifetime in the tension between truth and reality and untruth and unreality. This is the natural habitat of the mystic philosopher whose responsibility it is to experience the transcendental and accurately articulate the symbolism necessary for society to achieve order.

This Gnostic theme and the sickness of Western culture will be explored next. Gnosticism covers a lot of intellectual ground and will require a discussion of topics that include the definition of Gnosticism and its origins, deformations of reality, Gnostic thinkers, and symbols and language that are the battleground for truth and reality.

## 1.2 Voegelin's Definition of Gnosticism

### Voegelin's Evolution With the Term Gnosticism

A certain "tension of resistance" arose in Voegelin in his lifelong belief that there was a very serious and perpetual human spiritual problem in Western civilization. On a personal level this was characterized by a rejection of God as the basis of order, and belief in human efforts to achieve perfection equivalent to the Christian eschaton. At a nation-state level, this spiritual sickness had somehow risen to a highly destructive social and political mass phenomenon in the modern era. For Voegelin, this spiritual deformation led to a loss of truth and a lapse into unreality. Any movement to embrace a human order void of a spiritual basis and that seeks instead an intra-mundane salvation for man through human action was a phenomenon he dubbed Gnosticism (Rossbach, 2005, 78). The term had origins in antiquity and was most closely associated with a dualistic religion from the Persian region and some early Christians. Voegelin concluded the Gnostics primarily sought a release from the evils found in human existence and yearned for the eschaton or death to join God in a more perfect realm (Rossbach, 2005, 79).

Over his career he refined the term, its meaning, and its symbols in language. When examining the whole of his career, the picture that emerges is of a thinker who discovers a problem, but then struggles with its proper articulation. Voegelin does not seem to struggle with identifying the malformations of spirit and reality. Instead he struggles to find a linguistic symbol suitable to cover the entire scope of the rejection of the basis of order in all its manifestations. Throughout his career, Voegelin would repeatedly return to the Gnostic problem and wrestle with its meaning and implications. At a conference on "Gnosticism and Modernity" at Vanderbilt University in 1978, Voegelin said that he would probably not use that term if he were starting over again because the ideas he was referencing with the term Gnosticism included many other conceptual strands, such as apocalypticism, alchemy, magic, theurgy, and scientism (Webb, 2008, 49).

Most of what Voegelin had developed on Gnosticism by the release of NSP had come from works of the eighteenth, nineteenth, and early twentieth century's academics and theologians writing on various aspects of the phenomenon. By 1980, the studies of ancient Gnostic movements had moved light-years beyond what Voegelin could have gathered from his earlier research and they have continued apace ever since (Webb, 2008, 69). Not long before his death, Voegelin understood that historical research was revealing a very different concept of ancient Gnosticism and this had definitional implications for his original interpretation relating to modernity (Rossbach, 2005, 92). However, by this time he had developed the best articulation of the spiritual malformation he recognized in Gnosticism. This articulation came through in his final works as the relationship between symbolism and reality, which will be described later in this chapter. For now, it is important to recognize that while Gnosticism may be a controversial term, it does not change the fact that Voegelin was articulating something very real about the human experience: humanity does struggle with the problem of political order, its basis, and the rejection of this basis.

### History of Gnosticism and its Great Thinkers

Gnosticism is a fact of history. Its origins date back to the seventh century B.C. in the ancient Near East (Franz, 2005, 21). This region was wracked by a series of military conquests that profoundly disoriented the inhabitants of the numerous cosmologically-based (using myth to know man's place in the order of the cosmos) empires of the day. The violence, enslavement, and dislocation wrought by this wide-scale violence created a sense of meaningless and psychic disorientation (Webb, 2005, 51–52). It also introduced a forced intermingling of peoples and cultures that inevitably undermined faith in the traditional cosmological order. To comprehend the meaning of existence in this new and troubled world, three reactions are typically identified: stoicism, Christianity, and Gnosticism (SPG, 5–7).

The Stoics turned to a rational exploration of the world in a way that ushered in the advent of science, and turned inside themselves and experiences in the *metaxy* to discern the relationship with spirit. For the Gnostic man, the world appeared as neither well ordered in God nor inherently "good" (Webb, 2005, 51). This is diametrically opposed to the Judeo-Christian adherents who taught that what God created was essentially good and grounded in His order. In the ancient Gnostic view both the human body and earth were like a prison from which humanity was obliged to escape in order to return to "the other world of his origins" (SPG, 8). In short, the experience of the ancient Gnostics was of an alien, disorganized, chaotic, and meaningless world. God was a transcendent entity who was entirely divorced from mundane existence, which left this world devoid of reality. From this bleak outlook, the modern Gnostics adopted the belief that whatever salvation could be found for mankind could only come at the "destruction of the old world and the passage to the new" (SPG, 10). This new world could be achieved only through personal effort and a privileged "gnosis" of the means of escape. This "gnosis," a term derived from ancient Greek meaning knowledge, is meant to convey the special knowledge of a de-divinized salvation from a world where only man has the power to free himself from the mundane prison of his meaningless existence (SPG, 8).

Voegelin found the ancient Gnostic speculations significant because the experiences and beliefs they symbolize re-emerged out of antiquity and into our modern times with a brute force that indelibly shaped the modern era. His imagery for modernity was of a dualistic struggle between different representations of the truth of existence. On the one hand, truth of the soul and of man's relationship to God manifested in classical philosophy and Christianity was pitted against the "new truth" purported by modern "Gnostic" thinkers on the other. Ancient Greek philosophers discovered the truth of transcendent divinity in their explorations of consciousness. The methods, experiences, and truths they described were utilized by the early Christians to decisively differentiate the truth they found in the epiphany of Christ. The modern Gnostics held that the promise of a revolutionary transfiguration of man and society in time could be achieved through the radical immanentization of existence (NSP, 164–66). The Christian would find salvation through God, and the Gnostic through himself. The implications for order will soon become clear.

As Rome fell into decline, the Christian church was ascending. Political and spiritual powers were typically wed before the advent of Christianity, as found in both Greece and Rome. However, as the Christian church became the principal representative of the spiritual world in the fifth century A.D., it felt it must divorce itself from the political ruler as the supreme representative for both God and the state (NSP, 105). The church would now represent divinity and the state, man. Voegelin describes this event as a "radical de-divinization of the world" and a simultaneous dissociation of the previous unification of spiritual and temporal power. This situation held sway straight through to the Middle Ages as man's transcendent spiritual destiny was existentially represented by the Church, and the de-divinized temporal sphere of political power by the Empire (NSP, 106).

This schism created a challenge during the late Middle Ages by the rise of various "Gnostic" spiritual movements. Ironically, the seedbeds of modern Gnostic ideological consciousness stemmed from the desire to re-divinize the political society in the name of a new truth of existence. This time the threat did not come from outside Christianity, but from within as a division grew within the Christian community stemming from varying interpretations of the Revelation of St. John (NSP, 108). For certain early Christians this Revelation had aroused Jewish chiliastic expectations, and they were growing impatient for Christ's imminent second coming (NSP, 109). Sensing the danger in this problem, Augustine centuries earlier had set out to dash such expectations by re-interpreting John. Augustine declared that the thousand-year reign of Christ on earth had already begun with the Incarnation, therefore there could be no divinization of society beyond the *pneumatic* presence of Christ represented by His Church (NSP, 109).

Augustinian philosophy of history attempted to make it clear that the period following the epiphany of Christ was the last of six historical phases. This last age was known as the *saeculum senescens* (Age of growing old), and was a time of waiting for the end of history to be brought on through eschatological events. The Christian society must accept its *conditio humana* without yearning for the eschaton, and through the Church, realize a heightened natural existence given their ultimate spiritual destiny (NSP, 109). Augustine (A.D. 354–431) had also drawn a distinction between profane and sacred history. The sacred was embedded in a transcendental history of the *civitas dei*. It alone had direction toward eschatological fulfillment through the epiphany of Christ and the establishment of the Church. Profane history was merely waiting for the end in a radically "de-divinized" world. It had no direction and no meaning of any sort (NSP, 110).

By the twelfth century humanity was experiencing a growth in population and a civilizational expansion. Trade flourished, new settlements were founded, and with the rise of urban culture a renewed vigor flowed into intellectual life. This vital and expansive age no longer seemed congruent with Augustine's notion of a *saeculum senescens* (NSP, 110–11). New interpretations of history emerged to challenge Augustine's construction. Joachim of Flora (1132–1202), a Christian monk, developed his own interpretation of history by applying the symbol of the Trinity in a way that defined history (NSP, 111). As the time of the Father, Son and Holy Spirit passed, a certain phase of being would be seen in man, each one more complete spiritually. The Age of the Father traversed the beginning of creation to the time of Christ; the Age of the Son started with Christ and ended in Joachim's time; the Age of the Holy Spirit was about to dawn (1260 as it turns out) and would last as long as God wanted. The third phase would be a time of prophets, as men would no longer need the sacraments. This third age would culminate in the end of transcendental history, the Christian eschaton. This ontological transfiguration moved God into historical existence (NSP, 112–13). According to Voegelin, Joachim's construction is significant as it offers Western civilization a conception of history that is moving towards an intelligible end. This conception marks the beginning of the modern attempt to find a final end of mundane history that could plausibly substitute for the transcendental Christian end of history. Joachim's development of the three-age symbolism created a pattern for both the modern ideological construction of history, and the self-interpretation of modern Western society. This symbolism, and not the Augustinian notion, remains as the basic structure of politics to this day (NSP, 113).

The Joachitic notion of history had the ending of immanent history and sacred history coincide was a transfiguration of God. While St. Augustine found this notion entirely fallacious, it remained an entirely Christian notion. For many centuries after Joachim's conception, the new historical expectations he unleashed remained more or less within the Christian circles. Many Christians maintained the hope that the fulfillment of history would come about with an eruption of transcendental spirit (NSP, 119). As time progressed, Joachim's "fallacious immanentization" became more radical and the relation to transcendence increasingly tenuous, so that by the eighteenth century the meaning in history would be seen as a radically intra-mundane phenomenon. For Voegelin the result of this movement to non-Christian thinking is clear. As Enlightenment thinkers began to apply science to understand man, the idea of man's history as an intra-mundane experience took hold and ushered in the spiritual and temporal disorder and disorientation of the modern age. Its manifestation is the Gnostic (NSP, 120–21).

In Voegelin's *From Enlightenment to Revolution* (1975) one can see how certain Enlightenment thinkers picked up on the themes developed by Joachim and subsequent Christian philosophers, and in their new formulations, contributed to the "revolutionary" upheaval visited on the twentieth century (FER, 3). While Joachim meant to have an age transformed by the Christian Eschaton, in much the same way as John Calvin or St. Paul, it was the attempt to make perfection in the mundane world of the present that led Joachim to have some rather unseemly company in a philosophical sense (FER, 3). Voegelin analyzed Auguste Comte, Michael Bakunin, and Karl Marx. Each of these Enlightenment thinkers rejected Christian society, democratic government, and any philosophical leanings towards the transcendental. They proposed mass societies and revolutions to move beyond the social, political and economic structures of their day. Recent history has shown us mass movements' (National Socialism, communism) shortcomings as the basis for political systems, but Voegelin demonstrates why the philosophical underpinnings are equally as rotten. The absence of a transcendental relationship to "spirit," which is at the heart of each of the examined men's conceptions, leaves these conceptions with an inability to govern the ruler's passions or the people justly.

Voegelin's examination of Auguste Comte begins with Comte's positivism that seeks to replace God with the religion of humanity, and culminates in the failings of Comte's mentor Saint-Simone. Positivism proposes a social evolution that moves humanity from enslavement by traditional social structures and knowledge, then beyond God to scientific answers to explain existence (FER, 163). Comte's positivism concludes with a communal-style existence. Comte moves beyond the mere replacement of a governing system to the destruction of Western Christian civilization and the creation of a non-Christian society. Comte's views of both revolution and restoration are shaped by the French revolution. He felt the swings between violence and social reform, or the points of crisis, could be managed by "peaceful change" found in the power of reason (FER, 180). This reason would be administered by the intellectuals who would replace the Christian papacy with humanists able to provide the moral and intellectual firepower to keep this peace (FER, 181).

Voegelin felt Comte missed what the crisis was and the real issues of revolution and restoration. The crisis was the loss of spiritual substance in the ruling elites who lacked the courage to address social issues, and the lack of any usurping class to do the same once it seized power from the inept ruling class (FER, 181). Saint-Simone carried on the line of "Comtean" thinking about the "third stage of social progress" (communal) by the creation of a society that abolishes class by forcing everyone to work. All social value is derived from labor (mental or physical) and if you fail to obey the dictates of the totalitarian regime, you will be treated as a four-legged animal would be (FER, 192). As the "peaceful change" is managed through a series of ruling systems it will evolve to a government that dissolves into administration, and the crisis never returns—a fallacy that Voegelin explains as developed on poor philosophical underpinnings and an unrealistic view of human nature.

Voegelin deemed Michael Bakunin a Satanist and nihilist. Bakunin's philosophy of revolution rests on destruction. Bakunin is an anarchist and gives no real explanation for what comes after revolution or why (FER, 200). He detests Comte and Marx for their advocating a post-revolution authoritarianism. Bakunin saw Western history and social/economic structures with its focus on class domination and property as fundamentally evil. The ruling groups' domination and immoral treatment of the subjugated will ultimately lead to violent revolution. The real crisis of this age is not just in the treatment of the downtrodden, but in the utter absence of spiritual substance in Western society (FER, 233). In light of this spiritual and social decay, Bakunin's revolution is therefore the remedy and precondition required to destroy the institutions that sustain this sickness. The revolutionary process of total social destruction will lead to a change of heart by the survivors who will not make this same ancient mistake. To Bakunin, the revolution should destroy centralized power, as it is what robs man of social equality. Somehow, natural equality is preserved in this process. Bakunin makes himself the "Christ-like" redeemer as the lead agent in this destruction and redemption scenario, although he prefers to see himself as Satan giving Adam and Eve material knowledge. Bakunin-as-Satan gives the surviving society economic, social, and scientific freedom (FER, 231). Voegelin sees some strains of *metanoia* (transformation in turning towards God) in Bakunin's willingness to sacrifice himself for a better society, but that his concepts of the Russian and Western spiritual and societal history are defective which lead him to the wrong conclusions about revolution correcting the ills (FER, 231). Somehow, Bakunin misses the blindingly obvious point that any gap in control of a society will be filled by those brave enough to fill it (FER,

236). That simply cannot be purged from the heart of man because someone burned down the previous society. Societies collapse frequently, and often give birth to even more ruthless forms of tyranny.

Voegelin is at his best in demonstrating how Karl Marx's theories are both avoidant of certain types of philosophical inquiry and just flat wrong about revolution. Like Bakunin, Marx advocates revolution to transform and replace the social evils of the bourgeois-dominated social caste system that corrupts both man and society. Marx sees this period as a prelude to man's real history that begins when the old system reaches crisis and is destroyed. Man's heart and nature are changed by the resolution of crisis found only in revolution (*metanoia*) to the extent that a communal life based on equality will reign over society (after a brief interlude of authoritarianism, of course) (FER, 242). Marx spends most of his intellectual energy on explaining the deficiencies of the current society and steps leading to revolution, but surprisingly little by comparison on the form of government that results. Voegelin intellectually savages Marx for his failure to understand that the new society, now spiritually void and probably ignorant of Marx's philosophy, will simply fall back on the familiar patterns of history and return to the old society (FER, 246). That events kept derailing the predicted revolution, and no *metanoia* ensued once a revolution occurred, was to Voegelin proof positive of the inherent inaccuracy in Marx's dialectical materialism. Marx was simply not a prophet, just a man bent on describing the social injustice of his day and one prone to idle speculation of the results of so much suffering.

More importantly, Marx's flawed simplification of Hegel's notions of reality not only fails to explain reality, it sidesteps the totality of reality that includes a cosmic order and ultimately places man's meaning of life in the ill-defined consciousness of some "social being" (FER, 257, 263). That Marx was dodging the hard issues with a "big hand, little map" analytical process reveals a pathos in his thinking that Voegelin terms "logophobia," the fear of critical concepts (FER, 259). Marx's theories of the economy, history, society, and existence are conceived without the critical analysis required to actually have the basis of a theory. The absurdity of a theory without a theory would be comic if the consequences were not so grave (FER, 263). Marx's other great sin is to offer a gnosis that all human knowing of life and reality is a product of the intellect alone (FER, 267–68). Marx excludes the knowing of the soul or sprit as an independent or contributing factor in understanding reality. He sees God as a creation of the mind, and religion as a distracting force from understanding reality (FER, 267–69).

Comte, Bakunin, Marx, and Engels all make the mistake of believing simple reason can transform humankind to its highest potential without the transcendental guiding human morality with its "hidden hand" guiding moral order.

The Enlightenment offered man a new revolution in science and an ever-improving scale of material wealth, comfort and knowledge. Few things in human existence do not possess both negative and positive characteristics. Locke, Hume, and Montesquieu are part of the Enlightenment that benefited man in ways Marx, Comte and Bakunin could not. Voegelin felt that the movement away from God in the Enlightenment came to a dramatic high-water mark when Friedrich Nietzsche declared the "murder of God" (SPG, 39). This was the ultimate untruth that moved man and society from wholeness under God to the deformation of man ruling man as God. Unwittingly, the Gnostic thinkers' desire for a more equitable and just mankind without God left successive generations easily fooled by totalitarian formulas for achieving a utopian society.

There is a uniting theme in the various manifestations of this spiritual disorder, and Voegelin sees it in positivism, progressivism, Marxism, psychoanalysis, liberalism, communism, and National Socialism (SPG, 61). This theme is the radical "will to immanentization." It is the revolt against the transcendent dimension of human experience, which is the very basis of being. At their extreme, these modern ideologies not only reject the transcendent ground of being, they wish to eradicate the very notion of it and to replace it with a world-immanent order of being. This transfiguration of human nature would be brought about through human action in history and would enable humanity to build a terrestrial paradise that offers salvational qualities on par with the Christian eschaton. The phrase Voegelin made famous for this transfiguration was the "fallacious immanentization of the Christian eschaton" (NSP, 121). This modern conception of Gnosticism remains connected to its ancient past at the level of dissatisfaction and alienation found in human existence. While the ancient Gnostics sought a transcendental escape from the cruelty of life, the modern Gnostics deny transcendence altogether and seek human systems to achieve human perfection in some not-too-distant future (Sandoz, 2006, 149).

### Gnostic Definition and Summary of Goals

The modern Gnostics brought the Christian conception of man's ultimate transfiguration in God out of the transcendental realm and into the mundane. Humanity became transfigured in time, accomplishing this transfiguration through strictly human and worldly action. The transcendent Christian end of history became the mundane "End of History," which could be realized in the immanent future when man achieved perfection on his own. The various Gnostic ideologies took Joachim's notion of an end of history to a very different place than he would have imagined, not to a transcendental dimension of reality, but to a mundane one.

The evolution of Gnosticism was clear to Voegelin and as mentioned above, he recognized it in several different manifestations. Ultimately, Voegelin lists six characteristic features of Gnosticism. In *Science, Politics, and Gnosticism* (64) he states them very concisely;

1) Dissatisfaction with one's situation,
2) Belief that the reason the situation is unsatisfactory is that the world is intrinsically poorly organized,
3) Salvation from the evil of the world is possible,
4) If the order of being is changed,
5) And this is possible in history
6) If one knows how (gnosis is the knowledge of how).

Within this Gnostic definition, Voegelin emphasizes that ideological thinkers are not necessarily making a straightforward attempt to deny the truth of reality. Voegelin believes these thinkers are instead resisting reality or simply misinterpreting it. The Gnostic creators of ideological systems experience a reality that has an eschatological direction, a sense of moving beyond present structure, in a way similar to the philosophers and prophets that created stoic and Christian symbolism (SPG, 10). Although some may in fact be sensitive to transcendence, their *logos* resists its truth due to a lack of satisfaction in the present. Gnostics may believe reality moves both to a historical future and a transcendental beyond; however, the notion of a "transcendence into the future" points to a differentiation in existence they think best to obscure: that humanity can have an end in time without coming to a final End (*eidos*) outside the temporal order (NSP, 119). The *eidos* of history begins to loom as a major issue.

So just why would the Gnostic resisters push against a truth that, at least in part, they do not disagree with? What is in the human experience that makes this form of resistance a recurring force in history? As found in Voegelin's six characteristics, existential resisters are dissatisfied with the present human condition for its lack of order in personal and social existence. This is on many levels very understandable because human existence comes with a host of miseries that include but are not limited to hunger, hard labor, disease, enslavement and subjugation at the hands of others, early death, and the painful disorientation brought on by rapid change in the industrial and modern scientific eras (NSP, 120–21). Ideological resisters recognize and experience the suffering in the present disorder of man, and want to take action to resolve the maladies they see in the history of their own times. While they may apprehend a higher order, its fruits seem to lie beyond the possibility of realization in the present alienation. There is a sense of sharp disappointment with the slow pace of a transformational movement in reality toward the reward promised in the Augustinian notion of a transcendental beyond. The slow slog through history, and in their own lifetime, instills the Gnostics with moral outrage at the misery entailed by this snail's-pace movement towards an uncertain future (NSP, 122–24).

This sensible experience of moral outrage can lead to the conviction that something is fundamentally wrong with man's interpretation of reality. This belief moves the resister of disorder from morally offended to revolutionary as he now seeks to overturn the very structure of reality that seems so wrong. The transcendent is no longer experienced as an effective ordering force, as man puts himself in charge of his own destiny, which requires the ideologist to construct a system that will replace this ineffective basis of reality. Karl Marx offers the practical solution to the Gnostic problem of a divinely inspired reality in his Thesis on Feuerbach when he states, "Thus, for instance, once the earthly family is discovered to be the secret of the holy family, the former must itself be annihilated theoretically and practically" (Marx, 1845, 4). The end of human suffering and injustice in one's own time becomes the end of the normal human misery of history, and in effect, an end of history. Much like the eschaton, this new epoch will be characterized as blissful as man develops systems to overcome the sources of misery. Voegelin found this notion absurd. You cannot deny the divine nature in man while simply declaring an end to misery and make it so by the proclamation (NSP, 119–27).

There is, however, an even deeper stratum of resistance, one originating from the structure of consciousness itself and especially from its imaginative capacity. Imagination for Voegelin is the capacity that permits man to symbolize, to articulate and express, his participatory experience within the "metaxy of divine-human movements and counter-movements," the capacity that makes him a "creative partner in the movement of reality toward its truth." This creative imaginative force can go awry, however, if the creative partner forgets he is a partner and begins to regard himself as "the sole creator of truth" (NSP, 119–22). It is this kind of "imaginative expansion of participatory into sole power" that underlies the ideologist's illusory belief that he can create a new reality through creating a new image. Because of his imaginative capacity, man can confuse his image of reality with reality itself.

## 1.3 The Symbols and Linguistic Indices of Reality

### Symbols, Truth, and Gnosticism

As demonstrated, image and reality have a direct relationship. For example, the philosopher who captures complex experience and articulates truth through symbolism conveys truth to society. Voegelin believed that the derailment from truth begins with the degradation, loss, or misinterpretation of symbols of reality. It is therefore critical to understand how language, language indices and symbols reveal truth or the untruth found in Gnosticism. Voegelin considered experience to be the fundamental quality of human existence. Experience could be rational, mundane, or divine interactions, but no matter what kind or quality of the experience, it could only be realized in consciousness and represented by symbols. The symbols capture the essence of an experience and are thought to be true so long as they convey the original meaning of the original experience and continue persuasively to serve as full representations of that ideal in daily social usage. These symbols change over time as experience finds new expression.

Gnosticism is a symbol itself, or the articulation of a particular human experience that requires an interpretation of reality. As his research evolved, Voegelin attempted to better articulate the various forms of Gnosticism with language tools that conveyed the characteristics such as "egophany," "egophanic revolt," "pneumo-pathology," "*doxic* reason," "resistance to reality," "second ordered reality," "deformation of existence," "refusal to apperceive," and even schizophrenia (Rossbach, 2005, 89). These symbols of Gnosticism could be considered mundane in that they stand outside of an experience that is within the realm of conscious experience found in classical philosophy and Christianity, and therefore outside the realm where truth becomes illuminated. Aristotle used the symbol *ousia* (origin) to communicate this experience (A, 160).

However, using *ousia* in the present could lead to a problematic misinterpretation for a modernity that lacks an understanding of this essentially mythological concept. Even though accepted symbols are not the reality itself but a lesser approximation, getting them right and applying them correctly is critical to adhering to truth (A, 160). The *ousia* could work for modernity as a symbol as long as it is understood that it is not the reality itself. Rather, it is an image of a profound experience in consciousness, and the truth it represents is not a constant in time but the experience of truth at a moment in time. Understanding the nuances involved in the exploration of truth or reality is vital to forming a clear picture of why the Gnostic experience fails to achieve either of these forms of "knowing."

### Language Indices and Differentiation of Experience That Reveal Truth

In *Anamnesis*, Voegelin introduces the notion of "language indices" derived from the meditative process in what the ancient Greek philosophers called the *metaxy* or space of tension between life and death where the divine and human interact in the conscious mind of a human being (A, 103, 175). The language symbols that emerge from a meditative process are not objects or specific properties but are instead "language indices" arising from the *metaxy*. Understanding in the *metaxy* becomes luminous in the movement between the poles of divine and human areas of reality. In this movement between the poles, the experiencer becomes open to knowledge of reality previously felt as compacted (A, 176–77). This process of "knowing" truth is *noesis*, also derived from the ancient Greek, and describes the relation of order between the divine and human areas of reality. The language indices describe the movement in consciousness that illuminates both the process and the meaning within the experience. Indices and symbols derived from this process should not be understood as a "truth" to be clung to like an informative doctrine (A, 176). The truth found in the symbols is not meant to be simply informative, it is meant to define the truth found in the experience. The symbols are not references to structures in the external world; they are symbols of the existential movement in the *metaxy* from which they mysteriously emerge as the exegesis of the movement in expressive language that becomes intelligible by others who have not had this experience (A, 176).

A variety of symbols may emerge from the meditative process and can occur together in a cluster or group. These clusters or groups may form what Voegelin calls a "meditative complex" which is a "symbolic framework" where the symbols relate to and mutually illuminate each other (ISO, 56). Perhaps the two most important examples of these complexes are: "consciousness-reality-language" and "intentionality-luminosity- reflective distance" (ISO, 31–32). In *The Ecumenic Age*, Voegelin also mentions the complex "experience-question-answer," which must be taken as a whole to accurately describe the fundamental "constant of consciousness" of the human experience (EA, 75). Experiences in consciousness are multilayered and require a complex to capture the symbols of the experience of the *metaxic* tension. Because the complex holds the various poles of "tension" together as aspects of the metaphysical reality, consciousness becomes cognitively luminous in the experience (A, 177). The complex prevents the symbols from being misconstrued as separate entities, and creates a means to clearly communicate the essence found in the *metaxic* experience.

Voegelin believes that the components of the complexes are not to be separated or fragmentized. The full measure of the experience is only conveyed when all its constituent parts are expressed. The "tension towards the ground," a well-known Voegelin example, evokes a complex of three symbols (A, 175). There is a divine reality that inspires the soul's movement, a concrete human soul that quests for knowing, and the in-between of the *metaxic* experience (A, 176). The loss of any of these makes the experience of "the ground" undecipherable. This has implications on several levels, but in the modern scientific sense, Voegelin believes that the study of the divine side (theology), or the human side (anthropology), or the studies of the in-between process (psychology) are not endeavors to be conducted in isolation (Rossbach, 2005, 92). "The meditative investigation must not be deformed into these three forms" because "the in-between is not a question of psychology, theology or anthropology; it is always a matter of the response, of the movements and counter-movements" (MK, 43). Fragmentation can lead to the perception of a "second reality," where man is deluded about his nature, confused on how to seek knowledge, disconnected from his higher understanding of order, and easily manipulated into believing that there is no equality amongst mankind. In a sense, the "second ordered reality" is a symbol for man's modern state of confusion, and a key symbol to recognize when looking for signs of Gnostic influence (Rossbach, 2005, 98–99).

All meditative complexes emerge and unfold through a process of differentiation. As the meditative experience continues, new symbols evolve or old symbols take on new meanings and are either replacing or adding to the established symbols of truth and reality. New symbols represent a differentiation of the consciousness undergoing the meditative process and reflect a refinement of "vision" that enriches the language and understanding of truth and reality. As this differentiation unfolds, the singularity of a "compact" symbol is replaced with or augmented by the intricacy of a meditative complex (Rossbach, 2005, 96–97). The enrichment of a complex evolves into an index of the meditative process over time, and with the use of these complexes of symbols and their differentiation, the process becomes luminous for itself (A, 183).

These indices allow for the proper transmission of the special knowledge that comes from the participation with the ground of being in consciousness. The process of *noesis* does not reveal new knowledge about reality, but instead expands the base of knowledge from the compact material sense to the expanded sense as man breaks free of the strictly material and moves into the stream of knowledge available in the *metaxy* as his consciousness is drawn towards the divine (A, 183). The *noetic* gains insights into the nature of man, God, and the world through participation in consciousness with the divine and creates a logos through luminosity of consciousness itself. Knowledge is not changed, but the mode of knowledge is expanded as the material structure of consciousness becomes transparent and results in the correct assignment of symbols to accurately describe man's ground of being (Sandoz, 1981, 165). The Platonic-Aristotelian *noesis* (mental process of understanding from experience in *metaxy*) developed indices of science and theory in order to describe this higher mode of knowledge, and is distinguishable from the non-*noetic* beliefs and opinions about reality. Interestingly, Voegelin sees history as defined by the change in being we see through participation with reality in the *metaxy*, which in turn offers us meaning when we speak of political reality (A, 185). Political reality is the natural tension between the poles of the divine and the material. As we traverse the space between the poles we generate indices from the experience, and those become the autonomous objects of history and the history of ideas.

The experiencer of *metaxy*, usually a mystic philosopher or prophet, and the society that comes to rely on these symbols are in a state of tension. Voegelin emphasizes that *noetic* experience develops from the tensions within society and its conception of order. The *noetic* exploration of consciousness is always found where there is deep tension in society's self-interpretation. "The movement towards truth always resists an untruth" (ISO, 39). However, Voegelin recognized that truth and untruth, meditation and deformation, the meditative complex and deformation complex are not simply "opposed" to each other. He acknowledged that elements of untruth seep into the symbolization of truth and vice versa. Furthermore, the quest for truth can and has led to deformations and have contributed to the formative quest for the same as Voegelin states:

> a movement of resistance [against truth], if it achieves clarity
> about its experiential motivations and elaborates the story of its

deformative quest, can contribute substantially to the understanding of the paradox in the formative structure it resists, while
the defenders of the truth may fall into the various traps prepared
by their own self-assertive resistance and thus contribute substantially to an understanding of the forces of deformation"
(ISO, 39).

In opposition to untruth, Voegelin describes three fundamental symbolizations of truth that mark historical human understanding of the ground of
being found in consciousness: cosmological, anthropological, and soteriological. Cosmological symbols portray a society's institutions as a reflection
of nature, while anthropological symbols reflect the discovery of the individual psyche and its relation to right order that is beyond nature. Finally,
soteriological symbols indicate the experience of humans who encounter
divine revelation. By contrast, Gnosticism as its own symbol that charac-
terizes untruth believes that the Gnostic sage has achieved unity with the
godhead and thereby liberation from worldly human existence (NSP, 5). Instead of man and God working together in symbolic union, man is free to
reign in a universe void of spiritual unity. These two perspectives are irrec-
oncilable and deadly important to discern, which has made correctly defining symbols of conscious experience an animating force in Voegelin's
working life.

## 1.4 Chapter 1 Summary

Eric Voegelin found himself in the midst of a Western civilization tearing
itself apart. His ambitious philosophic endeavor was to deeply explore the
causes of this crisis and find remedies that could move Western man back
in line with the religious and philosophical traditions that had made it so
successful. Voegelin's was a quest to reveal truth and reality and to resist
the ideas and language of untruth. The truth of reality is that the basis of
order is found in the ground of being known to man only through conscious
interaction with the divine in consciousness. At the heart of modern Western
civilization's dramatic struggle to maintain its inherited understanding of
truth are the Gnostic attempts to replace these traditional truths with a new
formation for order that rejects any notion of myth or divine partnership.
For Voegelin, his personal and professional "resistance" to the untruth he
saw in Gnosticism required a much deeper understanding of the process by
which humanity comes to know the structure of reality and its attendant

symbols and indices. In Chapter 2, consciousness, philosophy, history, and the *noetic* and *pneumatic* experience will be explored. This exploration is the basis for the new science Voegelin felt was necessary to confront the crisis of Western civilization.

# CHAPTER II
# THE FLAME BURNS SO VERY BRIGHTLY

## 2.1 History of Western Truth and Voegelin's New Science

### *Western Civilization's Long Road to Truth and Descent to Untruth*

Voegelin viewed human history as a struggle to understand our humanity and to know our place in the universe. He believed that man's progress in achieving answers to the questions concerning human nature and order could be categorized by phases. Each phase was represented through symbolism that captured the essence of each historical era's struggle to understand existence and achieve order (NSP, 75). The recognition of a people as a distinct group is the symbol of "existential representation." Ancient societies saw themselves as part of a cosmic order, which is a symbol of "cosmological representation" (NSP, 76). As precision in assigning symbols improved, Voegelin asserts humanity achieved "differentiation." The next milestone of differentiation came when the ancient Greek philosophers re-imagined society on moral lines through the development of the psyche and discovery of the soul (NSP, 77). They used this knowledge to shape social and political existence under the demands of morality and justice. Voegelin calls this differentiation an "anthropological representation" (NSP, 77). Voegelin believed that the most complete articulation of the human condition to date came with the arrival of Christianity, which he thought provided even greater differentiation of the truth of the soul. With the advent of Christ, the soul is not only confronted by a divine standard of justice, but was transformed through God's initiative. This introduced "soteriological" symbolism into society, and paved the way for a new organization, the Christian church, to become the primary social embodiment of the truth of the soul (NSP, 77).

Voegelin gave a detailed chronology of how truth and order were discovered and then diminished over time in *The New Science of Politics* (1952). While humanity developed myths and symbols for order in the pre-modern era, Voegelin believes that the foundations for understanding order were not fully articulated until the Axial Age as sophisticated spiritual and philosophical schools were developed across China, India, Persia, Israel, and the Mediterranean. This was humanity's "great leap in being" (Sandoz, 2009, 8). In the East Asian civilizations, the Vedic Rishis, the Buddha, and Lao-Tse revolutionized how to understand reality and achieve social and political order (Sandoz, 1981, 118). In the West, it is the age of the mystic philosophers best represented by Plato and Aristotle who brought to the Western world a means to move beyond opinion and into "a way of being" (Sandoz, 1981, 118). Moses brought revelation, and Christ and his disciples a new way to relate to a singular God. In general, this "leap in being" did not shatter the primordial field of the "beyond," it dramatically moved man into it (IR, 10–11). Voegelin saw some equivalency in Eastern mysticism that was similar philosophically to the Greek and Christian practices, as both experiences brought insights into the "primordial beyond" that were original and of a similar quality (Sandoz, 1981, 118).

However, he felt the West offered a somewhat more differentiated experience in its relationship to order. The West's new philosophical understanding allowed for the rigorous exploration of the meaning of existence by elucidating the content of a definite class of experiences. The classical Greco argument is "not arbitrary but derives its validity from the aggregate of experiences to which it must permanently refer for empirical control" (NSP, 64). It is the period in which Hellenic philosophers discover the human soul through the intentional development of the psyche. These specially trained "mature men" (*spoudaios*) are the first to use philosophic methods in a scientific attempt to articulate the experiences their "soul" encounters in consciousness (NSP, 65). The class of experiences for the "mature man of character" includes the love of wisdom, the variants of the Platonic *Eros*, the *Dike* (justice), and the anticipation of death (NSP, 66).

As the progenitors of "anthropological representation" opened toward transcendental reality they "not only discover their own psyche as the instrument for experiencing transcendence but at the same time discover divinity in its radically non-human transcendence. The true order of the soul can become the standard for measuring both human and social types of order because transcendental experience represents the truth about human existence" (NSP, 67). This is not an arbitrary idea of man, or a theory about man, "but the idea of a man who has found his true nature through finding his true relation to God. The new measure that is found for the critique of society is, indeed, not man himself but man in so far as through the differentiation of his psyche he has become the representative of divine truth" (NSP, 67).

Historically paralleling the Grecian philosophic development, the Israelites experienced revelation, which led to the advent of Christianity. Voegelin believes that Christian theologians expand on the experiences of the Greek philosophers with regard to the understanding of human nature, and opening the soul toward transcendental reality. The Greeks emphasized man's ascent towards God; however, the Christians emphasize God's descent to man. If it is by philosophical reasoning that the *spoudaios* approaches God, it is by grace that God approaches mankind (NSP, 78). With the coming of Christ, "The critical authority over the older truth of society which the soul had gained through its opening and its orientation toward the unseen measure was now confirmed through the revelation of the measure itself" (NSP, 68). Voegelin's theory of political order rests fully on his assertion that philosophy and Christianity provide the basis for a critical judgment of the truth represented by society because "the substance of history consists in the experiences in which man gains the understanding of his humanity and together with it the understanding of its limits" (NSP, 78). Without the limits imposed on man by God, man is free to establish nothing more than man's own opinion and desires as the bedrock of social and political order. No matter how noble or sound, the "measure of man" will always lead to "demonic" ends in Voegelin's theory of order.

Despite its high degree of differentiation, the soteriological age was not without its problems. The rise of Christian symbolism developed in the Roman state came to almost entirely strip Rome of its former pagan sacral character. The head of state and the representative of the gods, always united under myth, separated with Christianity (NSP, 110). This was done at the direction of the Church leadership so that the Church could solely represent the divine order and the state could represent the profane order. There was no longer a "civic theology," so the interests of a temporal polity no longer had any mundane connection to God or one's soul (NSP, 159). Only the Church had this connection. This loss of spiritual-political union caused a revolt against the Christian conception of de-divinization of the state and created a Gnostic counter-movement to re-establish a divine order in a civil-theological wedded state (NSP, 107).

Voegelin traces the results of this divorce of civic and divine representation through time and, ultimately, to a surprising outcome in modernity. Beginning with Joachim of Fiore in the twelfth century, an attempt to re-divinize the political sphere sparked the Gnostic movement. As Voegelin explains it:

> Gnostic speculation overcame the uncertainty of faith by receding from transcendence and endowing man and his intra-mundane range of action with the meaning of eschatological fulfillment. In the measure in which this immanentization progressed experientially, civilizational activity became a mystical work of self-salvation. The spiritual strength of the soul which in Christianity was devoted to the sanctification of life could now be diverted into the more appealing, more tangible, and, above all, so much easier creation of the terrestrial paradise (NSP, 129).

The Gnostic utopia replaced heaven as the ultimate end of mankind, allowing any crime or tyranny as justification for achieving its terrestrial ends. The energy released by Gnosticism in pursuit of an earthly utopia may be credited with the rapid advances of the Enlightenment that formed much of the modern world. This energy can also be credited with eroding the foundations of traditional Western order (NSP, 131). The Gnostic counterfeit of the Christian eschaton debases and falsifies the truth of the soul, which in turn leaves man without a truth to know or a reliable basis for order (NSP, 121). It also gives the false impression of an *eidos* or end of history, when our humanly needs are fulfilled through human-based institutions that are capable of achieving some notion of perceived perfection (NSP, 121).

The dream of the Gnostic is to use the power of mass movements controlled by the state to transfigure the nature of man and thereby establish a terrestrial paradise that would be superior to the cruel and unjust world found under God (NSP, 132). When that dream is achieved, what you get is not paradise, but the modern totalitarian state. History shows that neither paradise is found nor human nature transfigured in this Gnostic quest. The result is typically a wholesale slaughter of all those who refuse to take the Gnostic dream for reality. For the Christian Western civilizations, God had been the traditional "equalizer" because man was created in God's image. The Christians believed God was in all men. This means that God is part of humanity's nature (*imago Dei*), and therefore all men must receive equal protection under the laws of society, which respects God's divine nature (PE, 192). In the Gnostic absence of God, man is free to make up whatever law he liked and apply it in a manner befitting the decision-making apparatus of the state (NSP, 162–63). God needed to be out of science, philosophy, and social symbols to achieve the Gnostic dream. Modernity continues to live in the soteriological era and benefits from the knowledge achieved in the anthropological and cosmological eras. However, the erosion of the traditional beliefs in the soteriological era is for Voegelin the heart of the Western crisis as he sees it.

Voegelin believed that with the removal of the divine from human nature, man's propensity for violence and widespread subjugation would reach ever greater heights. This makes the urgency of Voegelin's quest that much more palpable. Given his experiences with pre- and post-Nazi Germany, he knew that unreality could turn ordinary men into inhuman beasts. Since modernity long ago began to shun the metaphysical and spiritual relationship in understanding the field of human affairs, Voegelin recognized that modern science was inadequate to the task of understanding the truth that leads to political reality. He therefore catalogues natural science's shortcomings and proposes a new science that returns to its ancient Greek and Christian traditions. The remainder of Chapter 2 will be devoted to discussing the bedrock components of Voegelin's political science: the theory of consciousness, the *noetic-pneumatic* experiences, and how truth is political reality.

## The Problem of Modern Science and the Birth of Voegelin's New Science

Diagnosing the sickness of modern Western civilization and then proposing solutions was a monumental task. In the lifelong pursuit of this issue Voegelin developed an interconnecting web of ideas that included science, consciousness, God, man, society, governance, philosophy, and history to diagnose the Gnostic problem (Federici, 2002, 18). Voegelin came to the conclusion that social and political orders are entrenched in every dimension of human life. Man's nature, conception of reality, reason, and relation to the divine all lead back to the formation of social and political paradigms, which have been historically rooted in a divine order. However, separating these paradigms from the human experience of participation has proven to be nearly impossible. Viewed in this way, how else could Voegelin get to a truth about order and political reality without analyzing most of Western history, philosophy, theology, and scientific thought? More importantly, how could he as a scientist measure the experience of God or the search for order?

This creates a unique problem for natural science. Natural science depends in large part on an observer separated from the phenomena to be studied. In terms of observation, how can a researcher stand outside society and evaluate the basis for order critically or measure its relationship with the divine? Natural science is not well equipped for this problem and has shied away from addressing it (NSP, 2). Voegelin approached the problem using history to show how order emerged and then validated his findings through philosophical exploration of consciousness (NSP, 1). Plato and Aristotle would have felt at home with this process and would have found it scientific, but it is a process that natural science tends to reject due to observer bias and the lack of objectivity. However, if there is no separation between event and observer, there are few avenues to explore other than to have the experience. Therefore, exploring the experience and reporting the results are a valid form of study. God and order are experienced, both in the present and in history, so Voegelin analyzed both using ancient techniques that should be at least historically and philosophically valid (NSP, 3).

Voegelin concluded that modern science did not want to take on this thorny problem as it went against its largely positivistic ideology (NSP, 4). Modern science asserts that every form of science must emulate natural science with its mathematizing, particular methods, and self-imposed limits within material phenomena. However powerful this might be for the material world, it is not well suited for understanding man's nature (NSP, 5). Voegelin was very disappointed that modern natural science and its methods had become the exclusively legitimate criterion for theoretical relevance. He felt it missed the point that science was intended to aid man in understanding himself and his relationship to the universe (God), which is beyond math or the measures of natural science. For Voegelin, Gnostic-positivism has led science to accumulate often-worthless facts, misinterpret relevant facts, and to a methodology that precludes the study of all things outside the physical realm (NSP, 4). As a result, Voegelin believes that man has been misled about the truth of human existence.

Voegelin sees a human world where the sacred, once honored in every part of life and the source of morality and order, has been replaced by the profane (NSP, 6). This leaves man without moorings and drifting in an unjust and unstable world. In this anchorless modernity, the Greek philosophers and early Christian theologians have been so greatly diminished that humanity has come to think that individual opinions alone are the whole of truth with regard to existence. The exploration of humanity is still pursued; however, this pursuit is not to seek higher intellectual or meditative states that illuminate the truth through the mystical experience of the transcendental as has been the Western tradition. Instead, Voegelin believed natural science's human inquiry was used to immanentize man's earthly perfection through political and social systems (NSP, 10). This can only be achieved through the forced acceptance of the illusion of the unreal being the truth (man as sole source of reality) and the truth (God's reality superior to man's) of existence being unreal (NSP, 169).

Eric Voegelin sought to explore and rejuvenate political science and legitimize its philosophic roots as an indispensible part of this science (NSP, 2). He sought to revive the teachings of Plato and Aristotle and use them like a sword to cut through the veil of untruth sustained by positivistic science. Voegelin uses the problem of representation to illustrate how a restored political science could shed light on contemporary political problems in a way the political science of the positivists cannot (NSP, 5). To do this, he pushed scientific inquiry beyond the mere description of representative institutions, to what he defined as "the nature of representation as the form by which a political society gains existence for action in history" (NSP, 1). Voegelin believes that for each society, political institutions are founded on certain ideas. Constitutions and institutions could represent ideas well, but only for as long as they are beholden to them. For example, the U.S. Constitution, separated from its moral and philosophical concepts, would quickly become meaningless. Political science must therefore be able to discern the ideas that comprise the basis of society and its order. This was the intent of Voegelin's new science of politics.

## 2.2 Theory of Consciousness — The Key to Seeing the Way to Truth and Reality

### *The Ancient Past and a New Starting Point to Understand Humanity*

At the very core of Voegelin's political science, philosophy, and resistance to the destabilizing force of Gnosticism is his theory of consciousness (Sandoz, 2013, 57). Symbols that form society's notions of order, nature, reason, reality, and the divine are only concretely known through meditative experiences in consciousness (Sandoz, 1981, 156). This is the psychic space where man can shed his egoic state of being and inhabit his illuminated state of being. Man must base all that he knows on something, and that something is found in that internal space where participation with our psyche and higher nature can be accessed.

For Voegelin the act of participation in this experience is consciousness itself. His theory of consciousness is best expressed as a process of participation in the mind-space between material existence and the divine ground of being (Sandoz, 1981, 179). Voegelin's unique take on science and man did not spontaneously erupt in himself. It came to him through years of arduous study of history, myth, politics, religion, and philosophy. Through this study he came to understand what the ancient Greeks meant in their own descriptions of the human interaction with the transcendent divine being. This experience was at the heart of classical Greek reasoning for order. The study of man and nature was a scientific endeavor for the towering philosophic figures of Plato and Aristotle, who both felt that understanding the exploration of the ground of being was the *raison d'etre* for philosophy and science (NSP, 1).

For Voegelin's theory of consciousness, it was fundamentally important to develop a language that properly symbolized the modes of being, which would advance this science in a way neither Plato nor Aristotle had accomplished. These modes of being are 1) physical being in time and space, 2) mode of Divine being beyond time and space, and 3) mode of the In-between being which is the nonobjective reality of consciousness with its tension and dimensions (Sandoz 1981, 165). Because all that man knows of reality he knows through consciousness, science must ensure its comprehension of this medium of understanding as the basis for any scientific endeavor. Over Voegelin's career many of his ideas evolved; however, his theory of consciousness remained essentially the same from the late 1950s, and was best conveyed in his book *Anamnesis*.

In *Anamnesis*, Voegelin invites the reader to discover the concepts and methods of science that originated in ancient Greece. This foundational science was originally conceived to help humanity discover reality and know the truth about both our nature and the natural order conveyed in the experience of transcendental exploration (A, 33–34). Voegelin presents his core concepts on consciousness, man's nature, and reason that are highly evolved and historically grounded. Released in 1966, this book represents Voegelin at the mid-point of his career with a very full understanding of history, science, reality, soul, order and the shortcomings of each in our modern conception of them. Voegelin's gift is to remind us of what we have gained and what we have forgotten in our quest to know who we are and how best to live a human life in the company of others.

### The Anamnestic *Process and the Symbols of Truth and Reality*

It is not a simple process to understand consciousness or know how to study it. There are complications in how to actually move beyond "normal" experience and into the mental state required to develop an understanding of consciousness. Qualities of reason and meditation are needed for this exploration. One of the first problems faced by the scientist attempting to develop the faculties needed to explore consciousness is the conceptual "baggage" of his time and the dogma of his training (A, 7). A second is where to start, as consciousness, like history, has no beginning or end. Where do you decide to jump into this endless stream? Both of these problems dissolve with the understanding that there is actually no "I" that experiences consciousness and that the "flow of consciousness" is a similar illusion (A, 18). The quieting of the mind in meditation moves the experiencer beyond self-concepts and into the experience of being in the state of "experiencing consciousness." This is neither a label nor a concept, but a state of being. There is a sense of illumination in this state and the depth of concentration regulates the degree of control the experiencer brings to the process (A, 17). Practice is required.

Because this is a "knowing from within," Voegelin notes several problems. The first is that the experience of consciousness moves the experiencer from a finite to an infinite conception that lies beyond common language (A, 21). Using the symbols of myth became Plato's solution to give definition and meaning to the experience, although he recognized it was not possible to adequately define the infinite with finite language. Myth allowed for the excitement and wonder of the process to be conveyed to a wider audience who could more readily relate to the experience in this fashion. While Plato cultivates the effective myth in the *Politeia* and the *Nomoi*, Voegelin notes the problem of equality in relating the experience of the transcendental between those who know it and those who do not (A, 23). The most effective symbols once relayed to and instituted in society, become the basis of order (A, 24).

This gives rise to the second problem. Because the experience of consciousness is so vast and can be interpreted in so many ways, the myth can take on a staggering array of symbols. This is less of a problem in a pantheistic society, but wreaks havoc in a monotheistic society as adhering to one set of concrete symbols becomes very difficult over time (A, 26). As the base symbols become lost in the sea of competing symbols, the members of society lose the anchor of order and can feel lost in an incomprehensible world that seems to have no basis in order. The third problem is that of finalizing both a philosophy and a language that includes: theology, myth, transcendence of inter-worldly classes of being, and the ground of being itself. All of which demonstrate that the transcendent reveals the world as the immanent process of the divine (A, 27). For Voegelin, this was the only way to bring to the masses comprehension of the incomprehensible and the only basis for objective order of things in the world.

Two experiential complexes determine the resistance or acceptance of this philosophy and the language of symbolism. The first complex is "man's experience of his own ontic structure and its relation to the world-immanent order of being" (A, 27). This leads man to interpret himself as the basis of order and the ground of being. The second complex is obtained by using meditation to slowly illuminate the ground of being as divine in nature (A, 28). This process-theology is man struggling with the ontological questions that experiencing the transcendental gives rise to (A, 29). Clarity in consciousness structures is therefore critical for man to maintain order in the material world. Once the society loses touch with the truth in meaning of its mythical or theological symbols, which is inevitable, it must be willing to delve deeply into consciousness and renew or replace the symbols of order to move beyond the crisis of spirit. A new type of community must be imagined, or a rejuvenated older one, with concrete symbols derived from transcendental experiences that reveal the truth that man's ground of being is divine in nature (A, 34).

The ancient Greeks could see the truth and beautifully describe the crisis, but could never move beyond the concept of the polis to find a better solution for ordering politics and society. It was the Christian philosophers who took that step, using the *noetic* tools to plumb the depths of consciousness developed by the Greeks (A, 35). In *Anamnesis*, Voegelin demonstrates how a modern scientist can use the recall of his own "ah-ha" moments of discovery to cultivate a mental state of excitement that opens the door to higher states of consciousness. Philosophical inquiry can be generated in these states and directed to more specific questions by recalling specific types of memories. He details the memories of his own life experiences to demonstrate the process.

### Man's Nature Revealed

In *Anamnesis*, Voegelin follows his exploration of consciousness with a study of what is "right by nature" as configured in ancient Greece. Because of the incredible array of component parts, even Aristotle was challenged in laying out the best conception of nature. Voegelin insists that to know how to move towards an understanding of what constitutes nature in the Hellenic sense, you have to walk through the component parts and the confusion that ensues from the Greek habit of using the polis as the measure of all things. Once you have this worked out, you can then move on to how Aristotle dealt directly with the problem.

Voegelin distills the *Nicomachean Ethics* and *Politics* to explain Aristotle's formulations of the three fundamental definitions of justice and related phenomena (A, 56). These definitions are at the heart of explaining human nature, and include justice, right order, and judgment. As Aristotle outlined it, the first definition is justice (*dikaiosyne*) as it applies to a *politikon* (whose nature is to live in the city) (A, 56–57). Secondly, "right" (*dikaion*) is the order (*taxis*) of the *koinonia politike* (the political community). Lastly, the judicial decision (*dike*) is the determination of what is right (*dikaion*) (A, 56–57).

Aristotle placed the highest order of humanity in the *polis,* as this is where he felt human nature could best be expressed (A, 58). It is in the interaction between citizens where justice, right order, and judgment play out. Because humanity chooses a mostly communal existence, a collective agreement that both maximizes and/or restricts certain aspects of our nature is critical to maintaining order and our humanity. Beyond mundane (positive) laws, something more essential must govern what is just, which leads to the question of "what is right?" in the political sense. *Nomos* (law) is to rule, not the arbitrary will of man (A, 59). The ruler is to be no more than the guardian of the *dikaion* (A, 59). Justice is to be distributive and corrective between men who are free and equal. If the ruler violates the *dikaion* by acting in his own interest, he becomes a tyrant (A, 58). Confusion between these two laws leads to trouble. The justice of the polis is not positive law in the modern sense but rather essential law which gives rise to the tension between *physei dikaion* (what is just by nature) and the ever-present potential for making laws by arbitrary human will (A, 59). The *physei dikaion* is defined as what is right by nature in its tension between divine immutable essence and the human condition of mutability (A, 60). To maintain and protect order the society will need both divine law and mundane law, but divine law is always the highest order.

The issues that arise from this natural tension form the core of ancient political science as it attempted to answer the most important question for society: what is the right political order for society in a particular place and time? For Plato and Aristotle, the polis was the only model as they saw it as right, natural, and just. They never took it any further, although given enough time surely would have.

To help answer the natural question of political science, Aristotle offers the concept of *phronesis*. *Phronesis* is not a singular concept but a series of revelations that forces man to recognize that he needs existential power to mediate between justice that is permanent but also changeable in different situations (A, 62). Through meditation and the application of reason, the *spoudaios* go from general to specific facts of causation that reveals concrete action is a movement of being from God and ends in human action. This divine knowledge moves in us through knowledge, mind, and virtue or simply through *enthousiasmos* (A, 63). The wise man comes to a correct decision in this regard and the unwise does not. Our connection to the "unmoved mover in the cosmos" is the highest order of society. The *spoudaios*, who live in virtue and are not governed by their passions, are enabled to see the truth in concrete terms. Those who can act with effectiveness and simultaneously apply the virtue of correct speech about such action are said to be *phronimos* (A, 67).

Through this review of order and justice in the *polis*, Voegelin can more adequately address the question of "what is nature." Is man by nature an end or is he part of a larger order of reality? Relying primarily on Aristotle and Plato, Voegelin moves through some of the philosophical difficulties of answering the question in *Anamnesis*. Ultimately, Voegelin asserts that the act of being awake to the reality of order in man and the cosmos stirs the consciousness to recognize the cosmos as the background of thought and see the divine as the movement of being (A, 67). In man, the cosmos dissociates into an immanent world and a transcendent ground, but God and the world are united again in the experiences of love, faith, hope, desire for the good and the beautiful, and the turning toward the ground of being (A, 73, 80). Man enters into the known truth of his own order (his nature) through the experience of himself as the experiencer of order (A, 81). Voegelin includes the Hellenic notions, but both summarizes Hellenic philosophy and subtly expands it by placing humanity in the cosmos generally and not the *polis* specifically as a "universal humanity," instead of simply as a *politikon*. The *polis* offered a model for living with this philosophy for order; however, as Voegelin has described it, there is a more universal application that would be an acceptable basis for order in a village, *polis*, or nation state. This subtle shift was the influence of Christianity's *imago Dei* conception of humanity (A, 66).

This ontological complex makes sense only as a whole. Philosophy becomes senseless if it isolates man in a cosmos where God is absent. For the ancient Greeks, man is the questioner who explores the material world and his inner cosmos (in consciousness) in order to understand the human basis of order and the ground of being (A, 80). Our core nature then is found in the *noetic* experience of openness to the questioning knowledge and the knowing question about the ground found through the exploration of consciousness (A, 80). Through such openness, order flows into man's being from the ground of being. This stands in naked contrast to the Gnostic notion of man left alone to find order in a world without connection to the divine. Being, origin, and reality become critical points of delusion for Gnostic movements.

### *Being, Order,* Metaxy, *and Reality*

Just what is "being" and what is its "origin," and how can they be used to go beyond a dogmatic understanding of reality? Voegelin defines reality in Aristotelian language: reality is the very thing in which man participates. It encompasses all of the dimensions participating in the experience of reality entails, which includes the material, human, and divine (A, 163). It is the mutual interplay of these dimensions with each other in the operating sphere of spiritual, material, and conscious modalities. Being is the fact of experiencing the primary cosmic existence. The *noetic* experience is one of the highest forms of participation in the cosmic sense of being, as you most directly sense the ground of being which is the divine movement that moves humanity to obtain knowledge about the origin and from the origin (A, 80). Reality, the ground and order of being, comes from this *noetic* experience (A, 172).

This is hard to translate for the modern scientist who has no way to relate to this blend of logic and divine communication. For the classical *noetic*, the point of his philosophical endeavors was to "differentiate consciousness as the center of human order, in opposition to the cosmic primary experience and to the compact symbolism of myth" (A, 172). The dogmatic practitioners of modern science reject the *noetic* interpretation and claim only material being as reality and therefore, in Voegelin's estimation, have misinterpreted reality (A, 144). The modern *noetic* must therefore "re-establish consciousness in opposition to a dogmatism bare of reality" (A, 172). Voegelin saw this development of the rise and fall of *noesis* come to pass as a two-step process. First, the incomplete Aristotelian *noetic* vocabulary gave rise to the dogmatic reaction. The dogmatic reaction led to an inability to understand order in the ground of being and therefore an inability to know reality. To re-establish a connection to reality, the political scientist of modernity will need to move beyond scientific dogmatism and return to and complete the *noetic* works of the ancient Greeks (A, 172).

The Greek philosophers saw themselves as the lovers of wisdom who used reason to resist the social disorder of the day, and according to whom Voegelin styled himself in the modern era. The very act of resistance through reason gave rise to the *psyche* (soul) and the human *nous* (attraction to transcendental truth) or capacity for seeking true knowledge through transcendence (A, 89). Reason was discovered as both the force and the criterion of order. Plato and Aristotle realized that reason existed in human nature before its differentiation through first myth and then philosophy in the cosmologic and then *noetic* experiences of discovering reality through consciousness (A, 90). Unfortunately, this discovery would not prevent disorder. It can only help us resist the disordering effects of passion through persuasion. Between order and disorder, man lives in tension. Recognition of the proper symbols and qualities of this tension brought the philosophers to an understanding that the ground of being could only be found in the transcendental world, not the material.

Closures or obstructions to the "openness to the questioning knowledge" led to psychopathologies (A, 98). Cicero offered the best description of it: "As there are diseases of the body, there are diseases of the mind; the diseases are generally caused through a confusion of the mind by twisted opinions, resulting in a state of corruption; the diseases of this type can arise only through the rejection of reason; hence, as distinguished from diseases of the body, mental diseases can never occur without guilt" (A, 99). This turning away from inner knowledge (Plato and Aristotle's philosophic truths) led man away from the ground of his being and into confusion and disorder. This type of man has no understanding of his place in the cosmos and cannot relate to the notion of reason's ability to help place man in the unseen space between himself in the material world and God in the transcendent.

It is this very definition of this exploratory space in consciousness that one of ancient Greece's more stunning achievements is found. Somewhere between ignorance and knowledge the spiritual man moves in the understanding of his flawed nature and the perfection of the divine ground that moves him (A, 103). This is not empty space, but the pure realm of the "spiritual" where the human and the divine *mutually* participate in creating reality known as the *metaxy*. *Metaxy* is symbolized as the space between life and death. For Aristotle, the *noetic* life is the process of this experience of bringing the mortal to the experience of immortalization (A, 104). Man cannot achieve immortality in mundane existence, only in the space of the *metaxy* or possibly in actual death. This point has been often missed and became a source of misunderstanding, and the confusion between passions and reason could lead to disastrous outcomes and the passions often got the blame for the tumult that ensued in the misunderstanding. However, the misunderstanding of the *metaxy* and the desire for immortality in the present was actually attributable to the separation of both reason and the passions from their context in the tension between life and death (A, 104).

This distinction is important to grasp. The tension between reason and passion is an expression of our confusion in existing between the poles of life and death and human and the divine (A, 104). If a human being puts all of his energy into the passions, then he is consumed by them, but if he has only reason without passions, he will have no way to feel truth or humanity. Both are required and must be placed in context for the fullness of being to be experienced (A, 105). This experience of being is the relationship between the human and the divine in consciousness. Plato in the *Timaeus* beautifully captures this when he states:

> Now, when a man abandons himself to his desires and ambitions, indulging them incontinently, all his thoughts of necessity become mortal, and as a consequence he must become mortal every bit, as far as that is possible, because he must nourish his mortal part. When on the contrary he has earnestly cultivated his love of knowledge and true wisdom, when he has primarily exercised his faculty to think immortal and divine things, he will—since in that manner he is touching truth—become immortal of necessity, as far as it is possible for human nature to participate in immortality (A, 106).

For Voegelin, resisting the forces that lead man to pursue immortality in a human life, instead of in the transcendental truth found in Hellenic *metaxy*, was one of the most important insights of his career. However, despite the power of the *noetic* experience, Voegelin felt the *pneumatic* experience was even better at differentiating truth in the ground of being (EA, 305). Together, they could provide a potency of understanding rarely achieved elsewhere in human history (Sandoz, 2006, 129). To explain this unusual pairing, a further discussion of the *noetic* and *pneumatic* experiences is required. The next section will explain not just the space of consciousness, but also outline the actual tools necessary to engage in both understanding the experiences in the *metaxy* and the means by which to fully resist the positivistic influences on social and political understanding of order. This discussion will expose the truth about reality and the origin and ground of being.

## 2.3 *Noetic* and *Pneumatic* Experience—The Tools of Resistance

### The Ordering Function Found in Noesis and the Role of Myth

Voegelin's description of our ancient experiences in consciousness opens the door to a fascinating history of human exploration of our psychic space. The *noetic* developments of the Ancient Greeks were a major milestone in humanity's journey to understand our place in the universe and the basis of order for all mankind. This journey begins with man in a state of ignorance seeking to move beyond it. In this restless questioning he is guided by a ground of being that orients "man the questioner" to the ground and guides him to truth. This questioning yet guided sense to the ground of being was what Aristotle called *nous*. Because *nous* has several meanings in ancient Greece, Voegelin assigns the term *ratio* to help describe the directional nature of the ground of being. Voegelin's full definition of *ratio* is "the material structure of consciousness and its order" (A, 87). There is a mutual participation between the knower and the mover of the ground of being and the experience. To avoid confusion, Voegelin sets this as the primary definition of *nous* for the remainder of the book.

*Nous* retains two parts, human and divine, the knower/seeker and the thing that moves and gives knowledge to the questioning seeker (A, 85). Myth is never removed from the *noetic* understanding. In fact, *noesis* relies on a simple premise that is critical to creating truth in order: that all men are equally part of the essence of the divine, or in the *pneumatic* experience, God (A, 90). Without this premise, there can be no order and no ordering function for society, even if one does not know exactly what the divine is. Without the divine, *noetic* interpretation makes no sense (A, 86).

Plato and Aristotle recognized the "sameness" of the ground of philosophy and mythology in their own exegesis of the myths and the natural philosophical puzzles this gave rise to (A, 94). Voegelin lists eight mysteries to resolve in considering the impact of this combination. The first is that the space where the divine and human meet is the *metalepsis* and although there is more than one type of participation in this space, the philosophical inquest is one very particular type (A, 152). Second, a specific cognitive type defines the philosophical experience of *metalepsis* and the derived symbols relate objectively to the experience (A, 152). Third, generic logic in the *metalepsis* is the same material logic that explains the participation, the experience, and the process itself while actually being part of the process (A, 152). Fourth, *noetic* analysis can lead to the non-*noetic* experience being an object of *noesis* (A, 152). Fifth, the non-*noetic* can experience the *metalepsis* (A, 153). However, because of compactness and differentiation, the non-*noetic* will likely reject the divine in this experience. Once closed to the possibility of the divine, the non-*noetic* will not come to know truth with the clarity of the *noetic*. Sixth, the non-*noetic* objectification of the participation in the *metalepsis* yields a lower grade of knowledge of the ground of truth and the inability to recognize that the truth is the participation itself (A, 153). Seventh, one must have consciousness to participate in the *metaxy*. Knowledge derived from the participation can have degrees of truth based on where in the human timeline one participates (A, 153). Finally, the origin of history is human consciousness that knows the truth of the ground of being as a "quest for knowing" in which the participant participates from the perspective of mythologist, philosopher, or dullard if he is not beckoning the call of the question and yet still senses the calling (A, 153). The sum of these mysterious adventures over many millennia reveals a past, a present, and a co-tenancy in consciousness that defines history as man fluctuates in the "in-between" of *metalepsis* participating with the divine (A, 154).

As part of the *noetic* process, Voegelin identifies three types of Platonic-Aristotelian dimensions of consciousness: material structure, luminosity, and historical progression (A, 154). *Ratio*, the direction-giving aspect of consciousness, is the material content of consciousness (A, 154). The sense of questioning about the ground provides structure to myth and *noesis* and differentiates the conscious experience in participation to know higher from lower truth. The *aition* or origin of the unseen mover in the moved is the only truth of *nous* (capacity for knowing truth) (A, 155). The experience of consciousness and the degrees of transparency that one can know in interpreting the ground of being, are what Voegelin describes as the degree of luminosity (A, 156–57).

*Noetic* interpretation uses luminosity to make transparent past attempts to know the truth of ground and to know truth in the present (A, 154). This leads directly to the third dimension of consciousness and that is historical progression (A, 156–57). Without luminosity and *aition* there can be no knowledge of participation in consciousness and no knowledge derived from the experience (A, 155). This would leave no way to know the history of man's participation in consciousness. While man leaves physical clues to his having existed, Aristotle felt that man's knowledge was not left in these artifacts, but in the exploration of consciousness and relayed through articulation. This is what determines the historically relevant experiences from the mundane (A, 158). All experiences of the ground are events of participation, and the most ancient and cherished symbols from these journeys into consciousness will be our best hope to express that which is true in our present explorations of man's ground of being (A, 158).

The second critical experience in human consciousness came with the fundamentally original understanding of a singular God seeking a relationship with man. The *pneumatic* experience was born with Moses, but according to Voegelin was not perfected until the Christian philosophers united Christian revelation with *noetic* principles (Sandoz, 1981, 155). The *pneumatic* experience has the scientific dimension of *noesis* found in its philosophic underpinnings, but is probably more akin to the ancient human spiritual experience found in myth because daily spiritual practice does not have to be as rigorous as *noesis*. The enthusiasm of faith in the divine can assist the *pneumatic* practitioner in the *metaxy*.

Man has been compelled through the anxiety of existence to search for the ground of being and order throughout our known existence. The cosmological, anthropological, and soteriological phases of history are closely linked in that the relationship to the divine is the central component in establishing order (NSP, 76–77). Differentiation becomes the distinguishing mark, but that does not mean that the cosmological or anthropological phases were ineffective. In myth, we have a compact and undifferentiated conception of the divine that is accompanied with concrete imagery (Sandoz, 1981, 150). Cosmology was more than an irrational quest to understand mankind's place in the cosmos, as the exploration of asking questions about existence frequently led to pre-scientific forms of *noesis* (A, 152). Although often effective at various times, the symbols that were derived in this pre-*noetic* spiritual understanding could often be the source of error in the understanding of the true ground of being due to the lack of differentiation (A, 153).

In many ways, ancient Greeks such as Xenophanes and Plato and the ancient Israelites like Moses were reacting with horror to the mischaracterization of truth found in the symbols of their times (NSP, 69). A powerful truth that Voegelin makes clear is that although sometimes wrong, mythical symbols could be a true representation of the ground of being (A, 158). When those symbols were used properly, they provided a valid and productive understanding for society to base itself on (A, 158). In a very real way, man's quest to quell the anxiety of existence remains a mythical experience. It is simply more compact and less differentiated through *noesis* and revelation (OH, 7). Myth forged a path in consciousness still trod by the mystic philosopher, monk, or devout spiritual practitioner to this day.

## The Challenge of Maintaining Truth in Mythical and Christian Symbols

*Noesis* remained the West's "gold standard" of philosophical interpretation until Christianity unlocked the most highly differentiated and un-compacted truth of revelation. For all its brilliance and import, the *logoi* experienced by the sages of Hellas remained for Voegelin an essentially human wisdom (OH, 496). The *pneumatic* passion found in Israel and later Christianity is experienced, not as an act of man reaching out to God, but the experience of God reaching to man (Sandoz, 1981, 104). This experience turned the soul of man away from the world and society with its misleading notions of truth, and towards the source of all order and knowledge (Sandoz, 1981, 153). The Hellenic tradition traversed consciousness and the poles between man and God in the *metaxy* in a "push" mode. The Christians find God revealed to them in consciousness and are then "pulled" to the divine pole in the *metaxy*. The wisdom found in the revelatory experience became essentially divine.

The Hellenic "push" experience continued to slowly reveal truth and provide symbols articulating the ground of being and basis of order even though different practitioners could offer different symbols (A, 153). The effectiveness of a pantheistic system is that it allows for a more divergent use of symbols (A, 26). The prophets of revelation needed to be more accurate as they were all deriving truth from a singular source and therefore, conflicting symbols became more problematic. Although the *pneumatic* experience is vulnerable to misinterpretation in all the same ways as the *noetic*, the *pneumatic* prophets and apostles developed a specific sacred literature derived from a single God, which added a layer of complexity (EA, 306). Any conflict in interpretation of Christian symbols made reconciling these symbols challenging; a choice had to be made on which truth to follow (EA, 307–8). Additionally, the singular truth had a tendency to lead to a rigid religious practice over time. A rigid and dogmatic practice of religion runs the risk of moving society away from truth and order as the experience the symbols are meant to embody are replaced with the lifeless energy of dogma. Voegelin dubbed this process of loss or conflict in meaning of the symbols "dogmatomachy" (war of dogmas) (A, 199). Dogmatomachy can derail a society from its once-differentiated knowledge of the ineffable and lead to ideological movements that rebel against the now meaningless symbols of order (A, 200).

Unfortunately, modern experiences in the ground of being and its attendant symbols are a drastically reduced part of social and political "workaday" life. Voegelin notes that mankind moved on from the ancient Greeks and that modernity has diverged from Aristotle's exegesis (AR, 94). The cosmos once filled with gods and goddesses of antiquity, then illuminated by the God of illumination, has given way to a de-divinized world. Aristotle gave no language to a world separated into "that of things" and "that of space-time"; it was all one to him.

The immanent and the transcendent, and the mixing of gods and man, have no correlate in modern science. Aristotle's work was not continued in defining *metalepsis* or pursuing a *noetic* understanding of reality. A differentiated vocabulary was lacking that could explain modes of being and move the philosophic analysis forward. This lack of a common vocabulary and shared understanding of the origin of the material world led to the rise of what Voegelin called "dogmatic-metaphysics." For the dogmatists the material and spiritual worlds were differentiated and systematically separated. To the modern scientist, Aristotle was clear to mean physical stuff as "being" (existing) and its origin is something material, not divine (A, 160). The modern-day lack of clarity on this point became a point positivists exploited to further blur distinctions between form, substance, and origin to reject the reality established by Aristotle and Plato in the *noetic* enterprise (A, 161). The rejection of reality became the powerful core of ideologies and degraded scientific endeavor of the post-Enlightenment world.

Although controversial to Christians and scientists alike, the problems of dogmatomachy and scientism make clear why *noesis* is central to Voegelin's mythic philosophy and why he devotes so much of his writings to it. While the *pneumatic* experience brings a higher relation to order as revelation receives truth straight from the source, without the *noetic* framework to guide a human being through the experience in consciousness, the prophet and the society that depends on him for truthful symbols can easily lose their way over time (Sandoz, 1981, 165–66). Dogmatomachy results and ideological movements that are in revolt against some notion of a lost truth are given cause to flourish (A, 195). *Noesis* allows man to move beyond the structure of the world and see the pre-*noetic* truths in myth, the calling of man towards the transcendental, the dynamics of the *metaxy,* the need for accuracy in symbols and language, and to recognize the ground of being (A, 158). When paired with revelatory experience, the *noetic* process can reveal the truth of the divine ground of being and maintain a society in an ordered state for an indefinite period and at a level otherwise unachievable (A, 151). When not diluted by dogmatomachy, the symbols found in this pairing were what Voegelin believed to be the most highly differentiated and un-compacted yet discovered by humanity (Sandoz, 1981, 166–67).

### The Knowledge Revealed in the Noetic and Pneumatic Experience

The process of *noesis* does not reveal new knowledge about reality, but instead expands the base of knowledge from the compact material sense to the expanded sense as man breaks free of the strictly material and moves into the stream of knowledge available in the *metaxy* (A, 183). Luminosity increases as the participant propels (or is pulled) his consciousness towards the divine. The *noetic* gains insights into the nature of man, God, and the world through participation in consciousness with the divine and creates a *logos* through luminosity of consciousness itself (Sandoz, 1981, 166). Voegelin believed that knowledge is not changed, but the mode of knowledge is expanded as the material structure of consciousness becomes transparent and results in the correct assignment of symbols to accurately describe man's ground of being (Sandoz, 1981, 165).

The Platonic-Aristotelian *noesis* developed indices of science and theory in order to describe this higher mode of knowledge that is distinguishable from the non-*noetic* beliefs and opinions about reality (Sandoz, 1981, 165). Interestingly, Voegelin sees history as defined by the change or found through participation with reality in the *metaxy* —characterized principally as participation with the divine (IR, 10–11). This in turn offers us meaning when we speak of political reality. Political reality is the natural tension between the poles of the divine and the material (A, 145). As we traverse the space between the poles we generate indices from the experience, and those become the autonomous objects of history and the history of ideas (A, 176).

Platonic-Aristotelian philosophy and Christianity both empowered man as a contemplator of nature, and endowed man with the knowledge of himself and of order (Sandoz, 1981, 179). The Greeks recognized a need to place limits on human grandeur as evidenced in the *Eros*, *Dike*, and perspective of *Thanatos* as God-given limits and regulating abilities (i.e., love or understanding) for mankind (A, 34). The Greek tragedy was meant to symbolize the flawed nature of man, and aid in his coming to grips and accepting human limitation. Revelation offered a new form of relationship with the divine because of the notion of the divine reaching out to man. Seeking the life of the *spoudaios* was the model for the Christian clergy because this was a proven path to a transcendental beyond and provided a framework to understand that the individual knows freedom in the immediacy of God (Sandoz, 1981, 181).

Revelation is powerful when it opens the door to acceptance and love for the human condition and the suffering of man's fellows, which should thereby instill humility. Humanity has always lived in the tension of existing in the in-between state of the divine and the worldly (A, 89).

There is another form of tension inherent in the *noetic-pneumatic* exegesis process of experiencing reality and knowledge. Voegelin explains that as we interpret the triad or being-thought-symbol, we move from the exegesis as the reality of participation, to the reality that participation *is* knowledge (A, 144). The *noetic-pneumatic* exegesis lifts the logos of participation to illuminated consciousness by interpreting the experience (Sandoz, 1981, 185). The knowledge gained is therefore not abstract but direct and renders the *logos* of consciousness intelligible (Sandoz, 1981, 185). Ratio, love, faith, hope, spirit, and logos are interwoven into this knowledge. The complex of knowledge is differentiated through love of God and being moved by grace to always reorient towards the ground of being (Sandoz, 1981, 185). Man's existence is ordered by this knowledge (A, 184). The crux of this tension in reality and knowledge is found in the fact that *ratio* is only one aspect of knowledge in the field of possibilities of the conscious process of participation, and yet it is the thing that illuminates the structure of reality (A, 184). This simultaneously exposes the lack of truth in the non-*noetic* experience of this consciousness, and creates tension for those who sense it but may not understand it (A, 185).

This tension is shown in three phases. The Hellenic development of *noesis*, the Judeo-Christian tension in the *pneumatic* experience of revelation brought to *noesis*, and the Enlightenment "positivistic" philosophy that rejected the dogmatic approach to reality that had settled into Christendom over time (A, 186). This brings us back to the earlier-stated issue that modern science has lost the *noetic* knowledge and rejects reality as a result. The dogmatomachy issue is a rebellion against the reality it seeks to find using the now unreliable symbols developed in modernity (observer-material world-measurement) (A, 187). For the modern scientist to return to the state of knowledge achieved by the *noetic* practitioner would require him to lift the taboo of exploring the metaphysical and use mysticism's knowledge of reality. This would allow the scientist to establish concrete symbols that affirm man's return to the field of consciousness necessary to access the knowledge emanating from the ground of being and order.

### Voegelin's Exegesis Reveals a Truth Beyond the Empirical

Voegelin's scientific "truth" about human nature is that it can be oriented to both the divine and human poles of existence (A, 148–89). Unless a person has God reach out to them personally, *noetic-pneumatic* science will be required to moderate our existence and keep us oriented towards the divine pole in the *metaxy*. This requires time, attention, and discipline as we seek truth in the higher order of being found in the movement towards the divine. Man has to respond to divine initiative; the divine will speak the truth through silence in the *metaxic mystery* of consciousness for those who will attempt to listen (A, 149). Openness to the ever-present grace or mystery is required. In a sense, it is an endless journey with no final destination as we attempt to *know* God (universe, Brahma, Krishna, Allah, Nirvana, Christ). We can only *experience* the divine in our own presence in consciousness. No *end* should be made of it.

Through *ratio* and *nous* reaching towards the divine is essentially "natural" (A, 149). When the truth is revealed, the challenge is to adhere to the dictates of living in harmony with our fellows with love, respect, and compassion given our universally divine constitution. It is what the great philosophers of the axial age found to be the truth revealed in transcendental exploration (A, 150–51). No matter which pole we move towards, we walk with God (transcendence) as a constant either way. This means the option for *homonoia* (order through participation) is always available (A, 151).

Voegelin's *noetic* science can lead one to conclude a simple postulate: if man is the only legitimate basis for order, then man's hubris will dictate the terms of order. Without a higher order, the ends will always justify the means in our eternal search for order. Without a society willing to seek *metaxic* freedom and commit to equitable behavior for his like-natured kin, no lasting order can endure.

Taken from a modern natural scientific viewpoint, any inclusion of spirit, divinity, or God seems patently unscientific. Where is the proof? How can this theory be tested? The answer, as Voegelin pointed out, is that it cannot be empirically proven. This is science in the realm of philosophy. It is where the human experience of life has been explored for millennia. Voegelin's evocation of God is not religious—it is philosophical and existential. He is not asserting religious dogmas or creeds, but tracing the experience of man questing to find order in his internal, material, and social worlds. His form of philosophy is mystic in that it takes the tension toward the transcendent divine ground of being as the essential attribute of human reality as a fact and explores the whole hierarchy of being from this perspective. In practice, he is a mystic philosopher who uses *noetic* and the *pneumatic* experiences in consciousness as his primary tools to assist humanity in claiming its rightful place in a stable order of existence. This is a constant state of being, and will remain so as long as the philosopher and the society to which he belongs can resist those who move man away from this truth. This tension with seeking, finding, and resisting are well summarized in the following quote from Voegelin:

> To move within the *metaxy*, exploring it in all directions and orienting himself in the perspective granted to man by his position in reality, is the proper task of the philosopher. To denote this movement of thought or discussion (*logos*) within the *metaxy*, Plato uses the term *dialectics*. Since, however, man's consciousness is also conscious of participating in the poles of the *metaleptic* tension (i.e., in the *Apeiron* and *Nous*), and the desire to know is apt to reach beyond the limits of participatory knowledge, there will be thinkers—"those who are considered wise among men these days"—who are inclined to let the In-Between reality (*ta mesa*) escape (*ekpheugein*) them in their libidinous rush toward cognitive mastery over the *hen* [the One] or the *apeiron*. (CW Volume 5, 283).

## 2.4 Noesis and Political Reality

### Why Modernity Struggles with Recognizing Reality

Voegelin's critical analysis of modern science in *Anamnesis* offers a four-part explanation of why modernity struggles with the problem of political reality. First, he is pointing out what political science can and cannot do in answering the problem of political reality (A, 144). For Voegelin, modern political science does not include spirit in its analysis and devolves into dogmatism and ideology as a result. This defective form of science, unlike *noetic* interpretation, is not up to the task of determining political reality. Second, he is making the case that Aristotle and Plato laid the ground for a political science that, while not complete, offers the best means to answer the question of political reality through *noesis, nous, metaxy, logos, ratio*, and mythology (A, 112, 211). Third, he sees the loss of the *noetic* interpretation in modern science as the causal link to our lack of understanding of reality and the rise of dogmatic and ideological interpretations that badly misinterpret reality (A, 145). As always, he calls for a return to the *noetic* tradition and inclusion of spirit in defining man's reality and to provide the remedy for healthy social and political order. Fourth, he continues to discuss the need for symbols and improved linguistics to communicate experiences in consciousness. He introduces a new theme in the last few pages, common sense as the guide for the *human realm* (A, 207–8). He sees common sense as guided by *ratio* or *nous*, and critical in the practical application of *noetic* interpretation, all of which requires knowledge of consciousness and how to traverse it (A, 212).

Voegelin believed that, like truth, common sense in the human realm can only be applied once you have a level of mastery in the *noetic* exploration of consciousness (A, 211). He argues that consciousness is not some aberration, but is the concrete product of concrete people who order their existence in the world from the level of consciousness (A, 170). The quality of concreteness is seen in man's bodily existence that is the basis of social existence (A, 163). No matter the size of the society, an organizing ruler will be required to care for and defend the society. The form of organization this takes has been one of the principal driving forces in the study of modern political science. However, analyzing only *form* remains insufficient for the task of understanding political reality. At some point, you must understand the concrete experiences that gave rise to forms of order. The concrete consciousness has implications for both political reality and the interpretation of order.

Voegelin lists nine corollaries about political reality and the interpretation of order that naturally flow from the concrete consciousness (A, 200). The first is that a theory of politics must resolve the problem of order for the entirety of man's existence, while not obscuring sectors of reality, nor disassociating man's higher or lower impulses (A, 201). Second, man has only one consciousness to explore and that is the concrete one we have always known. Concrete persons can create a "social field" through shared and prolonged experience of consciousness and the habitual use of critical symbols. These social fields can define a society of varying size (A, 202). Third, social fields are not isolated to the society that generates them and one field can simultaneously belong to multiple social strata (202). Fourth, social fields generate the need to classify certain types historically and the civilization is the best unit of measure to use as a minimum field (A, 203). Fifth, the ecumenical field deserves its own category in the social field given its impact on modern ideology (A, 203). Sixth, the field of the ecumenical and the universal field of history are distinct. Concrete man experiences the conscious reality in his own time. The experience of ground might be universal, but it is only known at the time of experience. This is the distinction that makes history possible (A, 204). Seventh, universal humanity is not a field of potential organization but a symbol of it (A, 204). Eighth, history is an interpretive field (A, 205). Lastly, when man experiences himself as existing in both time and as a participant in the eternity of ground, he will have achieved optimal luminosity (A, 205).

This list of corollaries helps explain our modern interpretive troubles with reality. As modern Western civilization loses the traditional philosophic and spiritual symbols and means to know and sustain them, the symbols of order degrade. This occurs both in the present moment and over time. As the symbols degrade, they are replaced by ideological symbols that are not derived from the participating experience of *nous* in the *metaxy*, but in the mind of alienated men who no longer know the mystic philosopher's skill of interpreting reality. The ideologue can only explore the least luminous part of his mind and therefore cannot generate legitimate symbols of reality.

### How Reality is Observed

Political reality cannot be explained through direct observation. You must go back to the origin of the thing itself. It helps to understand Voegelin's logic if you define "political" as the *basis of order* and "reality" as the *nature of man* when preparing to explore this question (A, 144). Both the concepts of words "political" and "reality" can be further delineated as the desire for "knowledge of order" and the place where the truth of it is known "in the consciousness of those who desire to know" (A, 148). Therefore, political reality is found in the consciousness of concrete men who experience the knowledge of reality through the experience of seeking it (A 147). In that sense it is both a place and a condition. The very act of a well trained and properly oriented concrete man searching for the best order in society will find political reality in the very ground of being (A, 148). Interpreting symbols to explain the truth the seeker comes to know is where things can go wrong. Plato, Heraclitus, and Aristotle in particular developed ways to properly interpret this all-important "ground of being" (A, 164). Voegelin answers the question of what political reality is in several ways by explaining the process of knowing it, what the origin of the knowledge of reality is, how to get the knowledge, and how to know reality when you see it.

Voegelin is asserting that political reality is not just a description of events, the place where reality is observed, or the conditions of a particular time: it is a "knowing" (A, 163). Man's human experience with consciousness fosters order in organized society that can be deemed the *realm of man*

(A, 207). This realm is not measured through sense perception, but as a function of participation in consciousness. It is a realm that could be empirically defined by the historic level of *noetic* participation and the level of knowledge of participation derived from the exploration of the *metalepsis* (A, 208). No theory can deviate from these parameters in examining political reality. The model of *noetic* consciousness for the realm of man must include three principal characteristics. First, man's center of order must be founded on the existential tension towards the ground. (A, 208) Concrete consciousness is moved from the originator (*aition*), gives order to the organized society and related social fields, and is the basis of order for human and social history. Second, consciousness has a corporeal basis and runs through all of biology from highest to lowest with the power of organization running from the highest on down (A, 209). This consciousness is entwined with the divine and creates the pursuit of the good life of Aristotle and the existential tension that propels man to continuously seek out the divine. And third: man, society, and history overlap and fit together as the divine and material structure that is the *realm of man* (A, 209).

## 2.5 Chapter 2 Summary

Voegelin captures with amazing depth and clarity the path Western man took in discovering the truth of political reality through philosophy and theology. He also shows how the steady decline in honoring these traditions is creating a crisis for Western civilization. Despite the many gifts bestowed by natural science, it is not up to the task of assisting humanity with knowing the political reality necessary to sustain order. For Voegelin, a rejuvenation of traditional Greek philosophy and Christian moral and revelatory experiences is needed to stem the tide against disorder and inhumanity. Voegelin the "revolutionary scientist" diagnoses the problem and offers a means to understand both what we have lost, but also what we stand to gain through the *noetic* and *pneumatic* participation in consciousness with the divine *nous*. Voegelin offers the hope that there is a way to see, know, and experience truth as found in the order of being. Voegelin's analysis, theories, and new science show the benefits of reaching out to "know" political reality. Agreement on the basis of order cannot be systematized—it remains stable to the extent that the traditions and ideas of Western civilization that have been the bedrock of order, remain so. It is therefore vitally important to derive these "bedrock" ideas for order from the most fundamental truths we can know. Those truths and symbols only come from our experiences in consciousness and when accurately articulated, remain potent and powerful agreement on truth for many generations. This is a difficult task, but one that must be perennially undertaken. The crisis of Western civilization is the steady decay of truth in the symbols of order that are rooted in philosophic and spiritual traditions. These traditions are slowly being abandoned by Western man, leaving a gradually degrading form of order in some Western societies and distinct punctuations of disorder where the divine is replaced by man as the maker of order over others.

In Chapter 2 we have seen that Voegelin views order as a historical process and one that is defined not by physical action, but by human participation in consciousness. His quest and experience took him through an analysis of history, the inner workings of ancient Greek philosophy and mythology, the Christian and Israelite revelatory experience, and the process of science. The spark of passion ignited in the young Voegelin grew into a roaring fire by the time he wrote *The New Science of Politics* in 1952. This chapter has drawn heavily from both this book and *Anamnesis* to explain what he saw and what he thought needed to change. While we can see the framework of his argumentation, the full extent of his new science has only partially been traced. In Chapter 3, details on the mature framework of his *noetic* science will be provided, how his work can be applied in analyzing political reality, and a discussion of his critics will be included.

# CHAPTER 3
# THE FLAME IS PASSED ON

## 3.1 Voegelin's Revolution and *Noetic* Science Defined

### *The Shape of Voegelin's New Science*

Every civilization struggles with political and social order as it is a fundamental part of the human condition (NSP, 27). However similar the struggle,
the details vary across time. Voegelin recognized this truth and that he faced
different social and political challenges than Plato and Aristotle (NSP, 2). He
was looking out at modern humanity and seeing the insanity of mass movements spurred on by spiritless and destructive ideologies. From WWI, Nazis,
and the rise and dominance of Stalinism and Maoism, it was a world on fire
for most of Voegelin's life. It should not be surprising that a man of Voegelin's
intellect, ambition, and compassion was driven to identify and resist the ideas
that propelled mankind to what must have seemed like certain destruction.
It is perhaps harder to relate to his sense of urgency today because we have
seen the steady decline of these ideologically-driven mass movements that
once enveloped entire nations. They are not gone, and a few remain powerful,
as in North Korea and certain terrorist movements. For the most part, however, ideological movements such as communism and fascism have lost their
power to entice new followers. The remnants of these movements are evolving into something resembling old world oligarchies and thuggery rather than
maniacal ideological systems that will one day usher in utopia. Despite this
decline in totalitarian systems, the thrust of Voegelin's resistance remains
very relevant to modern Western civilization—identify the basis of order and
what will lead you to and from it (Federici, 2002, 21). The utility and appli-
cability in the form of resistance are therefore important.

As discussed in Chapter 2, Voegelin spent his career exploring all the
necessary avenues to understand truth, order, and political reality. He provided a remarkable amount of detailed analysis and theories on an incredible
range of topics. While his book *The New Science of Politics* offers the reader

a means to understand the problem of Western civilization's spiritual dys-
function as it both accepted and rejected order, Voegelin never sets out some
grand scheme to follow or dogmatic prescriptions to deal politically with
the problem of order (Federici, 2002, 183). Throughout his life he never ad-
vocated a return to some notion of a "golden age" or the intellectual acceptance of past symbols of order. His science was innovative and imaginative
because it was about a concrete person experiencing the present moment in
consciousness. Voegelin the revolutionary and revolutionary thinker are
what define his brand of political science because it is about the process of
knowing, participating, and being and not simply observing or following
the rules. This conviction to avoid a formulaic science meant that he never
set out simply to mechanically describe the sum total of his findings. Despite this, his "new science" takes on a certain characteristic shape that becomes clear through reading his major works. These characteristics are
much like a skeletal frame that society is encouraged to drape its "mental
flesh" around in the movement to understand the meaning of order found
in the experience of consciousness. This chapter will provide a clear picture
of the "shape" of Voegelin's science and how to apply it. While he produces
no dogma, one thing is crystal clear: his science is a call to action and understanding. Few acts are as important as resisting untruth.

### A Science With No Name, Gets One

Voegelin seems to view his 1966 book *Anamnesis* an act of resistance
in keeping with the philosophic tradition (AR, 73, 96). Voegelin was deeply
moved by the classical Greek philosopher's resistance to the decay of cosmological myth and rejection of reason in the Sophistic revolt of their age
(A, 113). For modernity, Voegelin felt what must be resisted is the "climate
of opinion" and "systems thinkers" that exist in a state of alienation from
the ground of being (A, 113). His strategic vision was to restore the ancient
Greek philosophical tradition as the centerpiece of a renewed political science committed to the study of humanity. He had four general goals to
achieve his strategy (A, 113):

* Restore the forgotten experiential milieu on which the meaning of rea-
  son depends
* Establish the inner coherence of scattered fragments of analysis
* Explore the pneumopathology of alienation and the derision of reason
* Portray the modern revolt against reason and the phenomenon of the
  System

Voegelin's new science was meant to restore the symbols of truth and reason, improve them, and articulate truth and reason through a revitalized and improved *noetic* political science (NSP, 31). The challenge of revitalizing and improving *noesis* was no small task. Voegelin described *noesis* as "the struggle in the *metaxy* for the immortalizing order of the psyche in resistance to the mortalizing forces of the *apeirontic* lust of being in time" (A, 112). This would require not just research and analytical skills, but meditative and spiritual ones as well. Voegelin's *noesis* is not a cheap imitation of the ancient Greeks, the Christian philosophers, or post-Enlightenment thinking. It is an amalgamation of all of these and something brand new. It is what Ellis Sandoz called *Philosophiae Homonis Principia Noetica*, in his 1981 book *The Voegelinian Revolution* (Sandoz, 1981, 188). While the *Principia Noetica* is in no way meant to be an exhaustive summary of all of Voegelin's works, it does offer a way to capture the essence and articulate the framework of what is Voegelin's new science of politics.

### The Fundamentals of the Principia Noetica

In the *Principia Noetica* concept there are no systems to adopt, axioms to follow, or laws to establish. Voegelin is asking us to continuously reach inside our consciousness and renew the ideas that bind our society to the truest thing about every one of us through the process of *anamnesis* and *noesis* (EA, 400–401). Voegelin's truth is that we are all share the same nature found in the divine *nous* (EA, 371–72). Therefore, society must accept that each member is to be treated equally under the laws executed by the political order (HG, 201–3). The social-political order must respect the unique expression of divinity that is the individual. Protection of all is a mandate in any society, but it must be balanced with the needs of the individual (HG, 228). The society is obligated to recognize truth and promote order that continues to adhere to the founding concept of order derived from the ground of being and symbolized in the *Corpus Mysticum* (HG, 202–3). Maintaining this balance cannot be the responsibility of the mystic philosopher alone. It is every member of society's responsibility to uphold truth (HG, 75). However, it will take the skills of the mystic philosopher utilizing anamnesis and skilled questioning in the *metaxy* to assist the society in maintaining its connection to the delicate tether of truth.

Voegelin's resistance was to the *libido dominandi* (lust for power) and the notion that a dogma or specific system would offer man salvation from disorder (SPG, 37). It was resistance to the notion that there is no divine nature of man and that man is the maker of order (SPG, 35–37). He was confounded by those who believed that truth could be known in static terms beyond the tension of existence and non-existence (SPG, 33). Like Plato and Aristotle, he simply would not accept the notion that we can ever stop asking questions of and about the "mystery" found in the *metaxy*.

Voegelinian political science utilizes the *via negativa* philosophical practice as its best means of articulation. Truth is to be constantly interpreted; therefore, it is better to say what the truth offered in the *noetic* science is not. This allows for interpretation in the present that is not forced into dogmatic terms or misinterpreted in a vain effort to see past symbols that no longer hold the same meaning of truth. Ellis Sandoz captured this very well (Sandoz, 1981, 201–2). The qualities of this *via negative* as described by Sandoz are (201–2):

1) The language used to describe experiences of truth in the *metaxy* must always be accompanied by descriptions of the context in which the enterprise is undertaken.
2) The language cannot specify a system, methodology, premise, or theory typical of modern science. The drawing of truth from the body of knowledge requires the meditative and directional qualities of the investigator, but the experience and knowledge found is utterly separate from a dogmatic means of its derivation.
3) Mathematics and physics are not to be used in *noesis*. This is a human experience in consciousness that is not bound to material measurement.
4) The philosopher's articulation of his experience does not constitute a fact. His words are representations that point to truth without fully capturing the entirety of truth. These words and ideas build a bridge for those interested in understanding the experience and act as checkpoints for those who wish to explore the *metaxy*.
5) The interpretation of the experience in *metaxy* as the experiencer moves between the poles of man and the divine is to be seen as incomplete. This is a process that relies on impressions and moments that glimpse truth, so the entire dimension of the truth can neither be static nor complete.

It was Voegelin's view that the *noetic* science of antiquity was derailed by the objectification of conscious experience and "doctrinalization" of the knowledge derived from *noesis* (Sandoz, 1981, 202). It is therefore imperative to remember that Voegelin's revolution was to insist that the knowledge of reality remain inseparable from the experience and the symbols derived in the participatory "In-between" state that illuminates knowledge (A, 152–53). The symbolizations, or language indices, that best capture this process are "consciousness-reality-language" and "intentionality-luminosity-reflective distance" (ISO, 13–18). Both of these indices capture particular aspects of participation, differentiation, and articulation. "Results" from these experiences must always be accompanied with the considerations that produced them. To do any less was an act Voegelin described as "butchery" that destroyed the reality of the experience symbolized (Sandoz, 1981, 203).

### The Epistemology of the **Principia Noetica**

Voegelin's *Principia Noetica's* epistemology can be broken into four basic sections: participation, differentiation, experience-symbolization, and reason (Sandoz, 1981, 204–14). These principles of discovery are the collective whole of the experience and cannot represent the experience unless considered collectively.

Participation is the central principle of *noetic* science (Sandoz, 1981, 204). It is the most fundamental experience of man in the material world (A, 206). Participation leads to understanding of "self" and one's place in the cosmos through primordial myth that captures human recognition of "spirit" participating in and undergirding reality. It is the mental, emotional, and spiritual interaction with the inner and outer world from which humanity can never go beyond to act as an external observer (Sandoz, 1981, 204). Participation has four experiential qualities: fundamental tension, hierarchy, question, and direction (Sandoz, 1981, 204).

The fundamental tension is the state in which man lives with the sense of being pulled to both the divine and basic human instincts that dwell in consciousness. Hierarchy is the sense of structure found in the questioning exploration of the *metaxy* of consciousness (A, 209). In the meditative and questioning state, the psyche senses hierarchy as ascending layers of reality as the experiencer moves from physical, to spiritual, to the divine sensorium (Sandoz, 1981, 204). The insight gleaned is of man's composite physical-divine nature, expressed as *nous* by Aristotle and Plato (A, 92). The "question" in participation is the never-quenched desire to know and explore the "mystery" of the ground of being (A, 92–93). It is the attuning apperception to seek out the truth of reality and the existence that seems to appear from non-existence (A, 93). Finally, participation is comprised of a sense of direction. As the name implies, direction is the sense of movement experienced in the *metaxy* towards the poles of human and divine being (A, 96). At a deeper level, it is the pull to the past to understand our beginning, to the beyond when moved towards the divine ground of being, to a sense of depth in the hierarchy of being, and to an end in the *pneumatic* sense as man is pulled towards the eschatological end (Sandoz, 1981, 205).

Differentiation is the second principle of the *Principia Noetica* (Sandoz, 1981, 205). In general, differentiation is the process in *noesis* whereby the experiencer learns to open to the luminous knowledge as movement towards the divine allows for the discernment of subtler forms of understanding of reality (EA, 314–15). Perception and apperception of knowledge, reality, and the order of being become more penetrating and complete as the experiencer becomes more adept at traversing the *metaxic* space and recognizing the changes in modes of reality in ascension towards the divine (Sandoz, 1981, 206). Differentiation is the act of knowing the difference between more compacted material reality and the expansive illuminated reality. In this act, reality is apprehended with the nature of man as a constant, the full dimension of human experience remains constantly accessible, and the structure of experience ranges from compacted to fully differentiated (Sandoz, 1981, 206).

Differentiation has two characteristics, knowledge and contraction. Knowledge is what is made available in the conscious-reality of the *noetic* process. This knowledge is of the illuminated structure of being, which remains as a constant and allows all men to participate through conscious reality. Dimensionally, knowledge grasped from consciousness includes the personal, social, and historical. Contraction on the other hand, is the movement away from knowledge, a closing to the openness of luminosity, and the rejection of the truth of the ground of being. Voegelin considered contraction the cause of the Gnostic derailment of truth as the ancient base of order was rejected (Sandoz, 1981, 207–8).

Experience-symbolization is the third principle in Voegelin's *noetic* science (Sandoz, 1981, 208). For the greater part of a given society, there is no meditative interaction with the level of conscious necessary to understand the luminous knowledge found in the *noetic* process (Sandoz, 1981, 208). The few who traverse this space can only convey the experience through symbols (A, 175–76). To the extent that the society accepts the truth of these symbols, there is social and political order (A, 176). Therefore, *noesis* is the process of having experiences in consciousness that garner truths that are then associated with effective symbols (A, 176). One needs the other and they cannot be separated. This unity stresses the cognitive and ontic process of experiences in consciousness as opposed to the subject-object model of natural science (Sandoz, 1981, 208). This unity is delicate and easily derailed as Voegelin asserts happened shortly after Aristotle's death and worsened over time. Interestingly, Voegelin notes that the long stretch of human history has produced many symbols (Sandoz, 1981, 208–9). Some mythological, some philosophical, and others theological, and yet despite their differences they can be equivalent (Sandoz, 1981, 208–9). This occurrence is less odd when viewed from the perspective that the same "inner *metaxic* space" in consciousness is constant and therefore, although experienced by many over many years and yielding different symbols, these symbols can hold the same precision of truth without being articulated identically because they are equivalent (Sandoz, 1981, 210).

The fourth and final principle of the *Principia Noetica* is that of reason (Sandoz, 1981, 210). Reason in the *noetic* science is the knowledge about human affairs known through the process of participating in the tension with the divine ground of being in *metalepsis*, and the subsequent critical analysis of this experience through reflection (A, 89–90). The truest expression of reason is what Plato and Aristotle referred to as *nous* (A, 89). Voegelin expanded on the concept and under his *noetic* science, *nous* refers to the capacity of man that thinks and grasps meaning and intelligibility (Sandoz, 1981, 210). It is even more than a capacity for apprehending intelligible patterns or structures in reality; it is also the source of order in the soul, the dynamism for reasoning and judgments that create resistance in the soul to reject disordering influences from the surrounding society (Sandoz, 1981, 211). In terms of human action, *nous* is both the power to apprehend intelligible order and the force that creates intelligible order.

*Nous* is much more and has a far greater history in the human quest for articulation and it is best to let Eric Voegelin himself explain it:

> The *nous* had attracted the attention of pre-Socratic thinkers, especially of Parmenides and Anaxagoras, in connection with their experiences of intelligible structure in reality. Parmenides had given the name *nous* to man's faculty of ascending to the vision of being, and the name logos to the faculty of analyzing the content of the vision. He concentrated the pre-analytical content of his vision in the non-propositional exclamation Is! The experience was so intense that it tended toward the identification of *nous* and being, of *noein* and *einai*: in the rapture of the vision the knower and the known would fuse into the one true reality (*aletheia*), only to be separated again when the logos became active in exploring the experience and in finding the suitable language symbols for its expression. From the Parmenidean outburst, the classic experience has inherited the *noetic* endowment of man (the Aristotelian *zoon noun echon*) that makes his *psyche* a sensorium of the divine *aition*, as well as the sensitiveness for the consubstantiality of the

human *nous* with the *aition* it apperceives. While Parmenides differentiated the *noetic* faculty to apperceive the ground of existence, Anaxagoras was concerned with the experience of an intelligible structure in reality. Could the divine *aition* indeed be one of the elements as earlier thinkers who were still closer to the gods of the myth had assumed, or would it not, rather than an element, have to be a formative force that could impose structure on matter? Anaxagoras decided for the *nous* as the source of intelligible order in the cosmos and was praised highly for his insight by Aristotle. Thus, from the side both of the knower and the known, the experiences of intellectual apperception and of an intelligible structure to be apperceived, having gone their separate ways, were ready now to merge in the discovery of the human *psyche* as the sensorium of the divine *aition* and at the same time as the site of its formative manifestation. (A, 94–95)

### *Charting the Depths of* Metaxy

This remains a complex explanation of the internal dynamics of reason, psyche, nous, the depths, and the divine from which they arise. Fortunately, Voegelin recognized the difficulty and in *Anamnesis* (114) developed a chart to better describe the relationship between these experiential phenomena of humanity.

| | Dimensions of Man's Existence | | |
|---|---|---|---|
| | Person | Society | History |
| **Divine Nous** | | | |
| **Psyche - Noetic** | | | |
| **Psyche - Passions** | | | |
| **Animal Nature** | | | |
| **Vegetative Nature** | | | |
| **Inorganic Nature** | | | |
| **Apeiron - Depth** | | | |

Hierarchy of Being

In Figure 1 we can see the basic design of Voegelin's diagram, meant to cover the broad scope of human affairs related to the knowledge of reality. The order of formation of the left column is from the top down. The order of foundation in the right column is from the bottom up. The order of foundation of the top row is from left to right. Reason is the focal point and Voegelin listed three principles found in his diagram in *Anamnesis* (A, 114):

* *Principle of completeness*: A philosophy of human affairs must cover the entire grid without hypostatizing any coordinate of it, thereby neglecting context.
* *Principle of formation and foundation*: The order of foundation and formation must not be distorted or inverted.
* *Principle of metaxy reality*: The coordinates determine the In-between of the *metaxic* reality, made intelligible by the consciousness of *nous* and *apeiron* as its limiting poles. The poles cannot be converted to material phenomena within the *metaxy*.

In a very real sense, the diagram is both a map and a decipher code for the unreal. Voegelin envisioned this diagram as an aid in assisting students to identify the opinions of Gnosticism as false theoretical propositions. Truth and falsity can be easily located on the grid. The *Principia Noetica* is plainly rooted in classical Greek philosophy. It does, however, include the *pneumatic* experience, which will be described next.

## 3.2 History, Revelation, and the *Principia Noetica*

### Voegelin Blends Greek Philosophy and Revelation

The remaining element of Voegelin's *noetic* science is the *pneumatic* experience and its place in the flowering of human consciousness in history. Voegelin desires a return of an advanced *noesis*; however, his improvements on Plato and Aristotle included the revelatory experiences of the Israelites and Christians (EA, 305). He recognized the chasm between the common conceptions of faith and reason and they could be disassociated into two distinct paths if they were not recognized as the equivalent experiences in the *metaxy* (EA, 306). They were simply expressed in the symbolism necessary to convey truth in their own space and time and differed in symbol only (Sandoz, 1981, 213). Revelation offered a more complete experience in that God reached to man and incorporates faith to transmit the knowledge found in the divine-human interaction (Sandoz, 1981, 212–13). *Noesis* formed the most articulate way to understand the process (A, 211). The combination showed the way to and means of understanding the knowledge of the divine order to the fullest extent yet discovered by man. Therefore, revelation and philosophy are not incompatible in the *Principia Noetica*. Voegelin best expresses his philosophical and theological blending in a quote from his early career: "Philosophy is the love of being through love of divine Being as the source of its order" (IR, 24).

Further exposition is required to describe this relationship. A fundamental piece linking these seemingly disparate concepts is found in the meaning of history (A, 208). The rise of *noesis* and events of revelation unfold in time and are spread to humanity temporally (EA, 306). This shapes history and gives it meaning. While the truth remains to be experienced, the meaning of each of these historical processes has been mostly contorted as humanity either did not understand it or rejected it in the "present" of their own time (EA, 373). In *The Ecumenic Age* (1974), Voegelin recapitulates prevailing threads of meaning in the web of events called history. Voegelin's eight dominant threads in history are (EA, 371–72):

1) The advance in consciousness moves from compactness in the cosmological experience to *noetic* and *pneumatic* modes in Israel and ancient Greece that are differentiated, philosophical, revelatory, and mystic.

2) These new Hellenic and Israeli modes of consciousness represented a new division in human history and impacted a huge span of cultures.

3) Imperial conquest brought about new ecumenic empires that reorganized older communities into ecumenical societies that formed a chain from southern Europe to China.

4) As the imperial expansion continued, ethnic cultures absorbed the *noetic* and *pneumatic* experiences and symbols. The spread of these symbols coincided with a simultaneous doctrinalization and dogmatization that obscured and deformed the original meaning.

5) The massive imperial expansion gave rise to a historiogenic myth about the place in history of empires.

6) Conquest of empires from Greece to Rome to China, accompanied with the spiritual growth of the Axial age, gave these empires the notion that their expansion had meaning for humanity far beyond that found at earlier village, tribal, or ethnic levels.

7) As these empires break up, there is not a return to the tribal and ethnic cultures of the past. The ecumenic empire's cultural imprint remains

and a new society emerges from the chaos with its own distinct perspective on the philosophical and spiritual outbursts carried from the Mediterranean, India, and China.

8) For Western civilizations, a variegated but essentially ecumenic sameness of consciousness carries on for millennia and into the modern era with its many deformations of the *noetic* and *pneumatic* experiences. Despite the many compacted notions, revelation continues to offer movement towards the perfection of transcendental fulfillment, out of time, and in line with the ground of being.

Voegelin sees a "leap in being" with the advent of revelation and noesis (IR, 10–11). The Axial age gives birth to a spiritual renaissance that fundamentally changes how man understands his place in the cosmos (NSP, 77). The spread of Christian revelation and Greek philosophy coincides with the huge movement of people as the ecumenical age spreads ideas, destroys and recreates cultures, and fosters a more universal understanding of consciousness than tribal life had previously offered (EA, 375). The deformations of the truths of *noesis* and revelation are a part of this history that bears the mark of Gnosticism (Sandoz, 1981, 230–31).

Despite the constant presence of deformation, it was the insightful events of philosophy and revelation that engendered the knowledge of man's existence in the divine "In-between" and the language and symbols in which knowledge gleaned in this experience was articulated (NSP, 156–57). These events mark an historical "before" and "after" and show man moving towards eschatological fulfillment out of time (A, 118). This movement towards fulfillment leaves history not as an endless succession of human lives and their acts in time, but instead what Voegelin believed was the ebb and flow of human experience of participation with the divine in consciousness (A, 124–25). This movement towards the eschatological fulfillment was the mark of history (EA, 6). The process of history was the draw of the questioning self towards the mystery of reality that was illuminated through experience with the divine that, as experience grew and was increasingly illuminated for those who sought it, was transfigurative (A, 126). The problems in history arose when man sought immortality by drawing the Beyond into this world, or making himself a God (EA, 302). In these instances, man closes himself to the ground of being and moves away from order.

The anxiety of falling into untruth and therefore disorder can create the desire for divine intervention to end any and all disorder for eternity. Plato kept the *theophanic* (interaction with God) experience in check by limiting the enthusiastic expectations that would distort the *metastatic* experience of the divine of his adherents (EA, 303). Reason's counter-pull of passion was difficult to negotiate and Plato always steered his fellow *noetic* practitioners to recognize that the experience of the divine should not overwhelm the entirety of the experience (EA, 303). The practitioner experienced the divine in consciousness, but that did not mean a new heaven and earth would be ushered into existence (EA, 303). Because the experience was real, "mystery" remained a tempting place of solace and distortion in the turbulent existence of ones times.

### The Pauline Vision of Christianity

Christianity had Paul as its primary truth seer, interpreter of history, and experiencer of the *metaxy*. The Pauline vision was of a "superior degree of differentiation" in Voegelin's estimation. Like Plato he had to contend with distortions of the interaction with the divine. Human life is to suffer to some degree. The thought of a paradise free of the bondage of mortal suffering led many Christians to long for death so that they could know the eternal joy and glory of salvation in becoming a child of God (EA, 305). There is a tension in revelation and Paul implores his fellow Christians to build their virtuous character by accepting the joyful endurance of the gift of mortal life. Paul explains in Romans 8:18–25 that there is existential order in man's patient acceptance of affliction in life and the joyful acceptance of this is sustained by hope, which creates a bridge to God that will sustain the Christian for the whole of mortal existence (EA, 304). Articulation from man to God need not be as perfect as in other forms of theophany for the *pneuma* of hope in the heart of one's soul will carry articulation enough for God (EA, 307).

Like Plato, Paul's reality moves in the *metaxy*; however, he is also subject to Christ's revelation in the flesh and the sense of being pulled to God (EA, 305–8). Voegelin described Paul's experience as a movement through "perishing" and "not perishing" as Paul travels from existence in the *metaxy* as a medium for reality with immortality as a goal and death as a minor incident along the way (EA, 305–6). Death is just a switch from imperfection to perfection (EA, 312). This "extended travel" beyond Plato's metastatic experience is propelled by Paul's vision of the Resurrection of Christ (EA, 308, 310). This is an event in the Divine-Beyond that reaches into the *metaxy* and transfigures the human experiencer, because the Resurrection means that the relation between the human and divine had been altered (EA, 313). A new covenant is made with man by God because with the Resurrection man is given direct knowledge of God's will to move man beyond the old premise "in Adam all men die" to the eschatological fulfillment "in Christ all men shall be made alive" (EA, 313). The Resurrection becomes the divine mythical symbolism for the transfigurative event as Paul attempts to relay the "cosmic-divine drama that begins with death and ends with life" (EA, 313).

The Pauline vision of death and resurrection is truly mythical in the same sense as the ancient Greeks (EA, 314). Christ is raised from the dead and with him all those who believe in him (EA, 314). He then destroys his enemies to include death and hands this cleansed kingdom to God the Father, who is now victorious over the rebellious cosmic forces (EA, 314). The symbolism is classical and dramatic; however it does create a certain amount of confusion as to when transfiguration would occur (Paul thought in his lifetime) and exactly how these events would unfold in time. Nonetheless, the triumph of Paul's mythic vision is that it is highly differentiated because it reveals the truth of God's love of man, and God as the "mover of theophanic events that constitute meaning in history" (EA, 315). Additionally, Paul offers not just a directional movement in the *metaxy*, but a specific aiming point and goal beyond the *metaxy* that is to be obtained as man returns to the imperishable state in union with God after death that is eschatological fulfillment (EA, 316). Perhaps most dramatically for mankind, it is in man himself where the divine fully expresses "Itself" in material reality and the site where luminosity gives its fullest expression. Voegelin believes that *noesis* is given its most full expression in Paul's exegesis (EA, 305). The powerful symbolism of this exegesis is of the humanity that achieves freedom from the cosmic fates by entering the freedom of God who redeems man through loving grace (EA, 316). God, who is also free from the dictates of the cosmos, differentiates the truth of existence that is now visible in the philosophers' experience that had previously seen transcendental limits (*athanatizein*) in the *metaxy* (EA, 315).

Despite Paul's revelation and expanded differentiation, there is still much agreement between the *pneumatic* and *noetic* theophany and its role in human history (EA, 306). Plato and Aristotle would agree with Paul that history is the space of reality where directional movement of the cosmos achieves luminosity in consciousness (EA, 306). Furthermore, all events in history are defined by theophanic events. Lastly, they would agree that the reality of history is that it occurs in the In-between space in the *metaxy* where man responds to the divine presence and this presence evokes a response in the participation (EA, 306). Outside of history, they agree that there is no subject or object in the experience in the *metaxy*, there is only the symbols of the human and divine. Man knows order in the divine ground of being, and that the rejection of these symbols means to reject the basis of order (EA, 306).

### The Spirit of the Principia

The interpretation of classical *noesis* and its limits, the *pneumatic* addition to classical *noesis*, and defining history by theophanic events are the major structural components of Voegelin's *Principia Noetica*. He points to the rich and complicated process of knowing order and truth and recognizing the rejection of it. Plato, Aristotle, and Saint Paul were pivotal historical figures because of the truths they revealed in their personal movement with the divine in the *metaxy*. Of course, time did not remain static and these experiences and symbolism were left to more than two thousand years of interpretation. For Voegelin, knowing the truth was as important as resisting the pull of those who reject it (A, 126–27). Educating mankind of his achievements was his calling, resisting those who denied the ground of being as the basis of order was his passion. In the *Ecumenic Age*, he gave the name *egophany* as the best-formed symbol for the state of alienation from truth and lust for power of those who rejected our divine heritage (EA, 327).

Voegelin's unique research style of personally investigating consciousness using anamnesis, studying law, learning and applying ancient Greek philosophy, learning several languages to read original texts in Hebrew and Greek, studying revelation, and staying abreast of current political issues with contemporary colleagues such as Hannah Arendt and Leo Strauss, and the tumultuous historical events of his life put Eric Voegelin in a unique position to strive for a deeper understanding of what brings order to man. Although he did not coin the term *Principia Noetica,* and would balk at attempts to narrow his work to a simple set of ideas, it is an apt way to describe the body of work his efforts produced.

If one reads a large selection of his books, it is impossible to miss Voegelin's obviously driven and cantankerous if not combative personality that seems so well suited for a revolution. It is also impossible to miss his concern for humanity and the fire that burned in him to pass on the knowledge he accrued in his search for order. His revolution was not a movement of bodies but of mind and spirit. He is the revolutionary who does not want to tear down social foundations like Michael Bakunin, but instead seeks to rekindle man's ability to live well in rightful order. In a sense, he seems more a kindred spirit of the Founding Fathers than Strauss or Max Weber. He passed this "fire" to his students and the world through his many publications, papers, lectures, and letters, not at the end of a gun or in elected office. This fire in the mind and soul is the structure and intent of the *Principia Noetica*.

Given the ethereal nature of his *Principia Noetica*, it naturally leads to the question, what do you do with it? Can this mystic philosopher's *Principia* be used for political inquiry in a fashion similar to other political theorists like Machiavelli or Weber? The answer is a resounding "yes" and will be the subject of the next phase of investigation of Voegelin the revolutionary.

## 3.3 Example of Voegelin's *Noetic* Science Applied

### *Hitler and the Germans: Voegelin's Application of Science*

It is perhaps hard to grasp how this philosophic thinker's *Principia Noetica* could actually be used in a practical analysis of the hardscrabble world of politics in reality. However, an example exists in Voegelin's diagnosis of the problem found in the relationship between Adolf Hitler and German society. Voegelin found a fundamental spiritual sickness in German social mores and institutions of the Hitler era (HG, 209–12).

Shortly after his return to Germany in 1958 to assume his newly appointed position at the University of Munich as the head of the Political Science Department, Voegelin decided a series of lectures was necessary to educate Germans on their societal culpability in the rise and support of the vicious cause of the National Socialist Party (Federici, 2002, 9). His analysis and subsequent lecture was later published in the book *Science, Politics, and Gnosticism*. Voegelin "overturned the applecart" in his condemnation of the German people. There were more than a few former Nazis in the audience and administration of the University. Voegelin, ever the pugnacious pugilist, waded in without hesitation. He was eager for Germans to realize and accept their culpability and willingness to believe in a second ordered reality (HG, 1). It was a warning for the world of just how the rejection of the ground of being could impact social and political order. Several other lectures that followed, the most damning of which occurred in 1964, became the book *Hitler and the Germans* in 1999, thanks in large part to the efforts of Ellis Sandoz (HG, 1).

There is a clear undercurrent of passion and anger animating this series of lectures. Voegelin's personal history of repression by the Nazis and the physical threat imposed by them will likely make this seem simply natural. However, Voegelin is intent on conveying the import and extent of the danger of blindly following an amoral ideology. In any case, he doesn't allow his anger to derail his central purpose. Voegelin analyzes the various dimensions of the "abyss" into which Germany descended which included the academic, ecclesiastical, and legal dimensions.

### The Just Ruler and Society

In the opening of his lecture series, Voegelin gives an account of how the memory of Adolf Hitler was treated in retrospect by the German public, news media, and academics. He identifies a level of dishonesty in the treatment of "Hitler the leader" and the public willingness to identify middle-class Germans with support for Hitler's more dubious programs. This is what Voegelin dubbed the "buttermilcher syndrome" (HG, 58). For the majority of rank-and-file middle-class Germans, it was easier to accept being fooled by the "political genius" than to admit to supporting a murderous racist set on world domination (HG, 58). A silence had fallen over Germany for those who lived through the National Socialist period. Trials of former Nazis, and some honest historical works punctuated this silence, but the silence told Voegelin that the sickness that gave rise to the Nazis must still be present (HG, 64–65). The Germans showed little signs of wanting to reconcile an amoral past. Socially, this was a real problem as this seemingly corrupt social morality would still be susceptible to malign ideologies if not confronted directly. Even in the Germany of 1964, the ideas that would sustain the basis of order were at stake (HG, 38).

It is in this analysis of society that we get a real sense of how to apply "God as the basis of order" notions in Voegelin's *Principia Noetica*. The first analytical treatment Voegelin presents is on the notion of time. A common notion for the "buttermilcher syndrome" was an "un-mastered" past and its manifestation in a collective guilt (HG, 70–71). Voegelin dismisses this notion. The only "time" to master is the present and guilt can only be an individual experience (HG, 74). Time in the present has a deeper meaning. As discussed, Voegelin believed that history (time) was not the flow of events but the "presence" of God (HG, 72). Mastering the present means to live in the virtue of placing "time under the judgment of the presence under God" (HG, 72). This was a human, not just German, problem. This idea was well formulated by Plato in the *Politeia* and the *Gorgias* as Voegelin explains:

To place oneself under the presence, under the presence of God, and according to that to adjudicate what one does as man and how one forms the order of one's own existence and the existence of society, that for Plato was an act of judgment. That means that man is always under judgment; hence the myths of judgment in the *Gorgias* and the *Politeia*. And because he is always under judgment, under the presence of God, in the sense of this "being-under-judgment" he must adjudicate how he acts and how others act and how this action brings about an order of society. For Plato, therefore, the judgment is above all the investigation of the not-being-present of the sophists as individual persons, and a not-being-present in the sense of the presence of the entire society insofar as it allows itself to be led and or- dered—that means disordered—by sophistic ideas. (HG, 71)

Accepting the presence of God, and therefore mastering the present, has an additional stabilizing effect for society. As in Ezekiel 18:1–5, the deeds of the father are his responsibility to bear (HG, 75). Successive gen- erations may not be guilty or responsible, but are obliged to deal with the consequences. Each individual is responsible for his/her own actions, and to act responsibly in the face of past or current social misdeeds. Therefore, each individual is obliged to be just (HG, 75). We each live in a society and elect representatives for the society in whatever form of political structure adopted. Whatever choices these representatives make, whether the individ- ual agrees or not, the consequences of these choices must be borne by every individual. As Voegelin says so very well, if you elect "imbeciles and crooks," you will bear more negative consequences (HG, 76).

The National Socialists and all of their acts had created the desperate need for certain contemplative reactions by the Germans (HG, 77). The most fundamental was not just how heinous the acts alone were, but what spiritual sickness existed in society that would elect murderous thugs as their repre- sentatives and then support them in their criminal activities for more than a decade? What is the "something" that was not functioning correctly?

Voegelin's analysis of this deeper problem begins with the conception of legitimate authority for the ruler as reasoned by Justinian (HG, 79). Power to maintain internal and external order is the basic function of the ruler. To use this power legitimately, the ruler must apply the law of "justice of ac- tion" in the society in the classic sense, not in the sense of positive law (HG, 80). This requires a man of religious consciousness who uses reason as an intellectual virtue to dispense justice. The ruler must also be a man of spirit who will be a "defender of the faith" in that he upholds the divine ground of being as the source of order. (HG, 80) In effect, to lead you must have power, reason, and spirit. Hitler, however, only enjoyed naked power without the reason or spirit required by Justinian (HG, 80). The German people turned their back on the *noetic* and *pneumatic* truth that human nature is the fundamental blending of reason and spirit and that order must include these notions or become something inhuman (HG, 82). The spiritual sickness was the loss of dignity for humanity as Hitler rejected God and reason. The German people themselves rejected God and reason by electing Hitler, supporting his cause, and then failing to accept the consequences of his and their collective choices (HG, 86–88). As the Germans turned their back on the divine ground of being, *nous*, and reason, they reverted to compact notions of being and devolved to an existence in a second ordered reality (HG, 87).

It would be easy to dismiss Voegelin's analysis as a case of perceptive hindsight. Is it not possible that Hitler had simply taken advantage of a starving, impoverished, and defeated people? After all, Germans had suffered the loss of WWI, financial collapse, and a dearth of intelligent and capable leadership. These are facts. However, the German people had also chosen democracy, and with it the choice to be responsible for their government. Democracy is founded on the notions of freedom of choice, speech, and conscience. It is, however, made practicable through courtesy, compromise, and concession (HG, 85). Aristotle's "middle way" is required to balance competing needs and the choice to employ this balance requires the wisdom to see it through. Although defeated in the 1932 election, Hitler was made Chancellor in 1933 through a ruthless "back door deal," and from there he was able to dissolve the other sections of the executive branch (Sandoz, 1981, 51). The elected Nazis in the Reichstag enthusiastically supported all of this. Not rejecting Hitler's illegitimate rise to power meant the restriction of speech, movement, property, representation, civil rights, employment, conscience, and loss of life for entire segments of German society. The ruthless imposition of ever-narrowing choices could be plainly seen with the abolition of the constitution as Hitler made himself dictator in 1933 (Sandoz, 1981, 51). He then cracked down on Jews, Poles, Gypsies, political groups and dissidents, academics, and any other groups that threatened his power or did not fit Hitler's idea of "societal good." Even if he did improve material conditions for those bloodline Germans in good standing, Voegelin felt these average citizens lacked both the wisdom required to sustain democracy and a weakness in spirit to resist the injustice meted out to their fellow citizens (HG, 85). In effect, they failed to take responsibility for the officials they elected and rejected the ground of being for the more earthly pleasures of comfort, pride, and power.

This leads Germans of the Nazi era to be what Voegelin described as both stupid and illiterate. Hesiod classifies men into three groups: those who think things through, those who listen to the wise, and those who neither think nor listen. Those belonging to the third group are called "useless men" and can cause society great harm (HG, 88). Voegelin would add that useless men form a "rabble" when they have neither authority of spirit nor reason and are impervious to either when advised or reminded to do so (HG, 89). Voegelin modifies Hesiod's model and applies it to the German society of the Nazi period. He revises Hesiod's groups to be those with human authority, those who can follow authority, and "rabble" (HG, 89). Those Germans who were "stupid" were those who had lost their ability to spiritually orient and with this loss, their ability to act with reason and spirit (HG, 89–90). As a result, they acted stupidly. This led to illiteracy in the sense that the stupid had lost their ability to characterize reality, understand and explore the ranges within reality, or articulate these ideas (HG, 90). Voegelin would consider even the most educated aristocrat who can write volumes an "illiterate" if that aristocrat is "stupid" and cannot understand and articulate reality (HG, 90).

Thus we can give Voegelin's bottom-line diagnoses of the German societal problem: the Germans had lost the ability to understand and articulate that the constitution of man is found in his attachment to God. When this is resisted and results in a de-divinized world, disorder and dehumanization will occur (NSP, 159). In classical Greece, the *spoudaios* (full men who participate in knowing and articulating the divine truth of order) were to be the elites of society who kept the tether of "truth in order" connected to the society (A, 65). Those unethically developed that might resist the truth as told by the *spoudaios* were thought to be "slaves of nature" (A, 69). For Nazi Germany, academics, clergy, and those who represented the law were supposed to be equivalent to the *spoudaios* of Hellas. However, instead of holding fast to the truth of order, they acted as "rabble" who further de-divinized and dehumanized the society. As these men led Germans further from truth, the disorder became worse. Truth gave way to "stupidity" and "illiteracy" whereby all manner of lies were accepted as men dwelt in their second ordered reality (HG, 97).

### The Academics' Failure

Voegelin sets out a scathing multi-faceted attack on German intellectual, social, and legal institutions that should have held sway against the clearly immoral dictates of the National Socialists and their supporters. As an academic himself, this idea of stupidity and illiteracy was especially noticeable within academia. Voegelin's principal example of this "rabble" is the historian P. E. Schramm, who edited Hitler's Table Talk (HG, 53). Voegelin derides Schramm for producing an "anatomy" of the dictator that reveals a fundamental lack of understanding of the man and his motivations (HG, 54). For Voegelin, this lack of understanding is reprehensible because the intellectual tools needed for correct understanding were available to Schramm who let Hitler off easy and never pushed Germans to explore the challenging questions concerning their support for Hitler (HG, 56–57). Schramm, and all of academia that excused the German people, failed to recognize the truth readily available to them in classical philosophy, biblical theology, and the writings of contemporaries such as Karl Kraus, Robert Musil, Thomas Mann, Hermann Broch, and Heimito von Doderer (HG, 98–114).

### The Church's Failure

In the general sense of being the representatives for spiritual transcendence of man, the Christian churches of Germany failed to spiritually lead the German people. Interestingly, in 1937 one percent of the population was Jewish, a small percent were not affiliated to any particular religion, and the rest (over 90%) of Germany belonged to one or another form of Christian faith (HG, 156). Therefore, there is no tension between the representatives of the state of Nazi Germany and the church-going peoples; they are one and the same. Voegelin notes that in this situation where the church participates with the corrupted political and social dimensions and is not in a state of resistance to an obvious moving away from God as the basis of order, it too is corrupt (HG, 157). The corruption within the church comes from a decline in intellectual ability within the ecclesiastical orders, protectionism of church-controlled interests, and lack of moral conviction that what the Nazis were doing was wrong.

He saves particular vitriol for German Evangelicals for several failures. The evangelical churches' lack of a central doctrine and extensively trained clergy left these mostly Protestant churches within a range of perversion of the Bible that ran from the radical to the relatively scant (HG, 1 58). Most fell on the radical side of the spectrum and preached anti-Semitism, German superiority as the chosen people, and the denial of political rights to those who did not fall cleanly into the German genetic and Christian categories (HG, 159). The most egregious miscarriage of Christian principles is the German Evangelical church instructing German parishioners to follow the dictates of Hitler as proscribed in Romans 13:1–7 "Fulfill your duties, tax where tax, tolls where tolls … honor is honor due" (HG, 178–83). Sadly, the Germans are only asked to follow Paul's instruction for new Christians to follow the dictums of Rome. Of course this was meant to instruct Christians of Paul's day to follow Roman imperial rule until it runs afoul of God's law, not to follow it blindly. Unfortunately, what the Evangelical leadership taught and what was believed was that if German law put whole groups like Jews or other undesirables outside the laws of God, so be it, for they are outside the protection of the sacraments (HG, 180). Their clergy did not instruct the Germans that if German law runs against God's law, they are not obliged to follow it. The German Evangelicals failed to follow through to the more important dictum in Romans where Christians are asked to "love thy neighbor as yourself as love cannot do evil to thy neighbor; the fullness of the law, therefore, is love" (HG, 180). In one fell swoop, the Evangelicals legitimated a moral abomination, rejected Christ's most important tenet, and condemned those outside the "sacrament" to sub-human treatment by the Nazi regime (HG, 180–81).

The Catholics were only slightly better as they too failed to be a moral beacon to the followers of Christ in a very dark time. The Church's acceptance of Hitler was less enthusiastic than the Evangelicals', offering more "go along to get along" than leadership, but still lacking in understanding of Christ's message (HG, 187). During the 1920s, the Catholic Church condemned the Nazis as incompatible with Christianity, but reversed course in 1932 and endorsed him when he won office (HG, 186). They had initially worked out an agreement where the Nazis would give the Church latitude to operate as it saw fit within the law. Of course the Nazis subsequently changed the laws and restricted the Church (HG, 187). As the war raged on, the Church was further curtailed and over time began to put up some resistance to this Nazi oppression. Sadly, the resistance was mostly for the sake of the Church and not for the sake of the dehumanizing treatment and murder of fellow citizens and at times, fellow Catholics (HG, 188).

There was a tendency for the Catholic Church to distance Jesus from his Jewish origin. The silence of the Church after *Kristallnacht* and well-known murder of Jews by the Nazis was deafening (HG, 192). This was tame in comparison to the denial of the horrors of the concentration camps. Like the Evangelicals, the Catholic Church was not prone to see God's law as applicable to those outside the sacraments (HG, 189–90). When it came to the Jews, the Church often gave the appearance of thinking dehumanizing treatment was a means of settling the old score for the Jews having murdered Jesus (HG, 191–92). There were Church members and clergy who resisted, some even lost their lives attempting to stop the dehumanizing treatment of their fellow citizens, but the Church failed to act in accordance with the *imago Dei* and God's law that flows from it. Like the Protestants, the Church helped support the illusion of unreality.

Voegelin's singular message for the Church and Evangelicals is: if you are going to be the legitimate moral authority, do not just wear the vestments; you must use your head and act with conviction to counter dehumanizing practices in the society as God's law demands (HG, 199). Voegelin does take the time to walk through ten points on the fundamental teachings of Christ in order to dispel any confusion the German clergy might have on what the Bible says and means. Voegelin's points are directly quoted below (HG, 199–200):

1) Arrogance anywhere near the Church is objectionable—and never more so than when it occurs in the name of the Church, or worse, as part of the Church herself.

2) By the grace of the Word man will be elevated above his nature. The word of revelation has not gone forth to give clerics and theologians the opportunity of debasing man below his nature.

3) Christ is the head of the corpus mysticum, which includes all men from the beginning of the world to its end. He is not the president of a special-interest club.

4) To be a Christian does not relieve one of the duty of being a human being.

5) It would be good to read the whole of chapter 13 of the Letter to the Romans and to think it over carefully. Whoever subjects himself to this discipline will lose the desire to quote the first verse on its own and, with that, to get up to political mischief.

6) It would be good to read the fourth commandment, "Honor thy father and mother," before asserting—as can be read in the pastoral letters of the German episcopate—that it commands reverence to the state authorities and obedience to their laws. Clerics and theologians, even when the Spirit blows in the direction exactly opposite to theirs, should at least not falsify the words of the texts entrusted to them.

7) This is related to the Erlangen opinion (restricting who is part of the church): Father of Gymnastic Jahn (proffered the letters) is not a church father.

8) In the Sermon on the Mount, Matthew 5:3, it says, "Blessed are the poor in spirit"; it does not say, "Blessed are the weak in the head."

9) Regarding the relationship between Christians and Jews; that verse of John Donne I read out to you in another lecture is to be learned by heart. I quote it once again—it cannot be quoted enough:

> Spit in my face you Jews, and pierce my side,
> Buffett, and scoffe, scourge, and crucify me...
> They kill'd once an inglorious man, but I
> Crucify him daily, being more glorified.

10) And as the tenth point, to learn by heart the prophet Ezekiel, chapter 33, verses 7–9 (RSV). I am speaking it out to you. God is speaking to the prophet, to Ezekiel:

> So you, son of man, I have made you a watchman for the people of Israel; whenever you a word from my mouth hear, you shall give them warning from me. If I say to the wicked, O wicked man, you shall surely die, and you do not speak out to warn the wicked to turn from his way, that wicked man shall die in his iniquity, but his blood I will require at your hand. But if you do warn the wicked to turn from his way, and he does not turn from his way, he shall die in his iniquity, but you will have saved your life.

That such a spiritually homogeneous people did not recognize the divine ground of being as the basis of order and collectively chose such debasing and violent behavior is surprising, but hardly unheard of in history. Faith gets tough in the face of fear and material instability. Voegelin points towards a truth well defined by Thomas Aquinas in the *Summa Theologiae* that the Catholics, Protestants, Orthodox, or any group claiming to represent Christ's message should know intuitively: Christ is the representative of the *corpus mysticum* (universal humanity) (HG, 201). Christ is the head of all mankind and no one church can segregate itself from the rest of humanity and claim to be the sole representative for Christ (HG, 202). The exclusion of the rest of humanity is the dramatic creation of the "other" and leads to dehumanization and disorder. The church, the very segment of society that is to remind everyone to be human, was in the German case encouraging disorder and the hate of one's neighbor. Instead of Christian values being promulgated, the church's backing of the National Socialists meant that Nazi social values were to "lord the day" and thereby be socially validated through sanction by a legitimate spiritual organization. The "rabble," the "stupid," and the "illiterate" did not recognize the inherent problem or its implications (HG, 89–90).

Voegelin believed that there is a high degree of differentiation of truth in both the revelations of Judaism and the story of Christ (HG, 204). The Judeo-Christian beliefs offer a powerful intellectual and spiritual forcing function to encourage individuals to seek personal responsibility and a "common sense" bulwark within a society to prevent derailment into base and inhumane activity (HG, 205). Voegelin recognizes this is not an easy thing to achieve and that within the Christian faithful only a few people at any given time will understand and live from the truth of a universal humanity (HG, 206). The same held true for the classical Greek philosophers and their *noetic* science. Very few understood or acted on the powerful truth discovered by their philosophers (HG, 207). This points to the very real problem of structure. Even if everyone agreed to treat others as themselves, what form of political structure should order take?

Voegelin is quick to point out that for all its innovation, the *polis* was limited geographically and structurally (A, 56–57). The political construct of the singular *polis* does not help you answer how to rule many cities at once. For Western society, law is the universal answer on how to provide justice and a republic the best structure to govern a large group of disparate and widespread people, particularly for the modern nation state. Classical Stoic law with its focus on human nature was a powerful aid to Greek political management (HG, 208). The Jews had the Torah and although it created laws to follow, it never proscribed a particular political structure because the tribal one was a given. The Christian attempts to adopt Stoic law were problematic as the concepts of the divine nature of man under the pagan Greeks were divergent enough to make Christian natural law based on revelation and its symbols problematic (HG, 208). Positive law and natural law often clash and are frequently seen as incompatible (TL, 387). No great political system, philosophy, body of laws, or social structure has yet overcome the inherent difficulty in maintaining order that exists in the tension of all these sometimes competing and sometimes complementary necessities (HG, 208). The Germans cannot be faulted for not having overcome this very human problem. However, their legal and political structures were arranged in such a manner as to make Hitler's move from elected official to dictator a fairly easy process and did nothing to prevent him from nearly destroying the German people.

### The Rechtsstaat *and the failure of Law*

Voegelin is highly critical of the German political and legal system known as the *Rechtsstaat*. The *Rechtstaat* is the body of legal thought and organization historically tied to Germany and rests on the notion of a nation-state founded on a constitution where governmental action is restrained by law. There are problems with the German conception of separation of powers, which branches of government are empowered by the constitution, and who develops and imposes certain forms of law (HG, 215). As an example of the continuously poor state of German jurisprudential ability, Voegelin points to the Federal Republic of German's 1964 constitution, which is so poorly worded that it creates contradictory separation of powers and an easy path for the judiciary to fall under full control of the executive and legislative branches (HG, 216–17). The Weimar constitution was similarly flawed but made irrelevant as the basis for law in Germany as the National Socialists simply ignored it by 1933 (HG, 218).

The German legal scholars of both past and Voegelin's 1964 analysis believed in creating a legal hierarchical structure whereby each lower layer would fall under the next higher, with the ultimate source of all laws being the constitution (HG, 217). This is all well and good, unless the constitution is poorly written and leaves the development and enforcement of law to a branch of government, such as the executive, that could easily manipulate the law for its own ends. The poor state of German legal scholars' moral and intellectual center during the National Socialist era is evidenced in their quick acquiescence to Hitler's demands for rule without a constitution and support for clearly immoral, and what should have been illegal, acts (HG, 225). This was compounded by the legal imposition of harsh punishment in the courts for failing to follow Hitler's dictates (HG, 225). This derailment of law was compounded even further when the petit bourgeois that controlled various departments issued laws and regulations in pursuit of supporting the Führer, but were disconnected from any particular legal structure, moral code, or jurisprudential experience (HG, 219). Power was law, not any notion of Greek or Judeo-Christian law. Reason and spirit were once again sidelined.

Historically, the basis for German constitutional legal framework is positive law, although elements of natural law can be influential (HG, 225). Positive law is concentrated mostly on the acts of citizens ("thou shalt not" of criminal law), and not on pivotal moral issues as in natural law that would tend to be more applicable in civil matters or legal theory (TL, 378–79). However, when the constitution is geared towards positive law, it can become isolated from the ideas it is supposed to be founded on in its protection of human rights (TL, 387). Therefore a morally healthy society is necessary for positive law to remain viable. If moral decline is evident, then the state of the legal system is in jeopardy. In what could be considered a negative feedback loop, the morality needed to sustain the basis of law and order is reason and spirit, which is exactly the requirement for morality. If society is either not spiritually led or rejects the notion of spirit (and therefore reason) as connected to law and order, then only one conclusion can be made: there can be no law and order (HG, 226). Or as in Nazi Germany, if the entire society acts illegally, then there can be no *Rechtsstaat* (HG, 226). Law must be based on certain moral and logical premises for it to achieve its *raison d'etre*. When it is not, it is the sign of moral decline and the loss of order one could predict using the *Principia Noetica*.

In Nazi Germany law and order were supplanted by the exercise of power (HG, 228). Voegelin concedes that if this meant it was simply an authoritarian state, it might be acceptable as there are times when a single central authority is necessary to ensure survival, such as during a natural calamity or when certain levels of primitiveness demand it. (HG, 38) A typical authoritarian state can be brutal and restrictive, but they tend to focus control on those areas that either threaten or enrich them (HG, 221). The people may be told what to do to a lesser or greater extent, but not so much what to think. But the National Socialist government was not simply authoritarian, it was totalitarian. Totalitarian systems are much more repressive of pluralism and political rights than authoritarian ones. Under a totalitarian regime, the state controls nearly every aspect of the individual's life. Totalitarian governments do not tolerate activities by individuals or groups, such as labor unions, that operate outside the goals of the state. Law in Nazi Germany was not the foundational principles that morally guided the government in providing for the common welfare; it was simply a tool to be manipulated in supporting its own demented cause of world domination (HG, 38). The loss of the law was socially acceptable because Hitler was to bring Germany salvation through dominance.

Hitler, then, was no simple swindler who sold the Germans a false bill of goods. The Germans' moral decline made supporting Hitler seem natural. Of course terror, coercion, and fear were widely used along with high-quality propaganda. Some resisted outright, and some quietly. However, they collectively failed to see that dehumanizing tactics were in violation of what should have been their fundamental orientation as Christians and people of a democratic nation: that all men are God in the flesh and all must be afforded the basic rights and protections afforded under this simple moral precept (HG, 228). Murder is a violation of God's law, no matter the quality of propaganda attempting to convince the average German that Hitler's sanction of it carried more weight.

### The Truth in Order

Voegelin's *Principia Noetica* offers a powerful truth. Political order will be unjust if not founded in moral truth, and that truth comes from our universal transcendental reality (HG, 229). Blocking this from the mind leads to living in a secondary reality (HG, 240). In this reality, anything is moral as long as man declares it and believes it. For Voegelin, the death of the spirit left German society in this "secondary state" where it lacked critical judgment and an ability to resist what was dehumanizing (HG, 244). Voegelin traces the birth of the "secondary state" to Nietzsche's announcement that God was dead and that He had been murdered. In Voegelin's worldview, the men who sacrifice God to secular civilization constantly commit this Gnostic murder (HG, 240; SPG 39–54).

Germans did see Hitler as the savior who would usher in a German age of world-immanent perfection. They failed to recognize the Gnostic delusion that the more fervently human energies are thrown into the great enterprise of salvation through world-immanent action, the farther the human beings who engage in this enterprise move from the life of the spirit (SPG, 82–87). Because the life of the spirit is the source of order in man and society, the very success of a Gnostic civilization is the cause of its decline. The further the decline, the tighter the grip of the "second order of reality" becomes (HG, 255). Ordering the systematic extermination of Jews becomes simple logic in this state of being. Jews are outside the perfect German group, are therefore a threat, and under decree of the *Rechtsstaat,* as non-Germans they are outside the law (HG, 228). For order and human perfection in the world under a great German leader to be achieved, Germans have a moral obligation to eliminate the Jews. This will bring order and a utopia will follow (*immanentization of the eschaton*). If the Jews were seen as equally part of God, and God's commandments the basis of law, the Jews could never be seen outside the law (HG, 228; SPG, 63–68, 83–87).

There is ample evidence that the Nazis manipulated Germans through the use of science to prove the validity of their racist ideology and the "su-perman"-like status of the German people (HG 266–67). The Nazi race the-ory that claimed to be scientific, complete with catalogues of skull measurements as proof, is a good example. Academic and philosophical claims of the "death of God" are found in Nietzsche, Hegel, and other Ger-man philosophers, which only compounded the "spiritual" difficulties of the times (SPG, 39–40). Additionally, in the National Socialist coinage of a "Third Reich," there will be a "Thousand-Year Reich," which is to connote something permanent and unchangeable in an almost biblical sense. There-fore it is easy to see why an "end realm" would seem valid in the material sense to your average German before and during the Nazi era, but the es-chaton would certainly not seem transcendental. The use of science to prove German superiority, Christian terminology to appear spiritually sanctioned, and mass movement techniques to dilute individual autonomy are the hall-marks of the Gnosticism Voegelin rebels against. Contrary to the scientific method, the "powerful person" (Hitler) never invites his followers to test the rightness of his doctrine on their own or see any other god than himself. This is the pneumopathology of alienation writ large and demonstrates a clear divorce from reason and spirit. Hitler promulgated "truth" in the mode of absolute authority, which to Voegelin was the unquestionable power of *gnosis* (HG, 255).

Despite imperial roots, the loss in WWI, economic calamity, and soci-etal dislocation, the Germans did attempt a liberal-style democracy before succumbing to the ideological doctrines of the National Socialists. While an authoritarian regime probably would have been widely accepted given certain German cultural tendencies (*anstand*), it is the lowly state of moral order that best explains why both German society and its organizational in-stitutions so fully embraced the amoral and totalitarian ideology of the Na-tional Socialists (HG 58–59). It was not Hitler's dynamic personality, economic ruin, or a particularly evil German nature that opened the door to National Socialism. Voegelin concluded that the Germans' rejection of God as the basis of moral and political order left them vulnerable to the dictates of an all-encompassing ideology (HG, 55, 58, 89–90). The events surround-ing this moral decline were just aspects of the historical milieu in which the society had to respond.

### *Applying the* Principia Noetica

Voegelin used the considerable skills he developed over a long career to enable himself to look deeply into German academic, religious, social, and governmental entities and perceive a spiritual sickness. The pneumopathology of Gnostic alienation from the divine left the Germans susceptible to a maniacal ideology that sought power for power's sake. The society was led poorly by its elected officials, clergy, and academics, all of whom should have sounded the alarm that the direction the society was moving was dangerous and destructive. The Germans turned their backs on their responsibility as a democratic people to resist the darker inclinations of their representatives.

As Voegelin makes clear, the state, academia and the clergy actually avoided the responsibility to be just and instead readily moved the society to a second ordered reality by adopting the untruth that debasing and maltreating their fellow human beings was acceptable and even honorable behavior. The promise of utopia through a mass movement was the delusion the Germans believed offered salvation. In achieving this "salvation" all manner of dehumanizing and unlawful practices were acceptable because the state, religion, and academics endorsed exclusionary and discriminatory spiritual, moral, and legal practices. There was nothing within the German society to resist this movement towards immorality and sub-human existence because they had placed their faith in one man, not in the divine ground of being. As the *Principia Noetica* makes clear, God is the only thing man has to resist the "mortalizing forces of the *apeirontic* lust of being in time" (A, 113). In the rejection of the divine *nous (ratio)*, there is very little to prevent man from relenting to a darker nature that feels alienated and yearns for the bliss of not suffering within the "present" of a human life (SPG, 85). This is the desire for "immanentization of the eschaton" that offers the false hope of a mortal peace on earth. No sacrifice is too great in this pursuit. This is the pneumopathology of Gnosis.

If one uses *anamnesis* and develops the ability in consciousness to enter the *metaxy* to know reason and spirit of the divine *nous (ratio)*, then rejection of a man-made utopia will be a simple matter of common sense (A, 211). Voegelin's political theory is not a dogmatic system, but the constant process of defining reality through conscious participation in the *metaxy* and using the *metaxic* knowledge to interpret the reality of a given day as Plato and Aristotle did. In the process of living, the *noetic* should live in the knowledge that life is a gift and we honor the sacred when we respect it as St. Paul taught. There is little evidence that in the Nazi era of Germany, the citizens experienced the healthy *Principia Noetica* factors of participation, distinction, experience-symbolization, or reason, and ample evidence that they did not.

## 3.4 Chapter 3 Summary

This chapter has offered a consolidated perspective of Voegelin's "new science" and how to apply it. Ellis Sandoz's description of Voegelin's *Principia Noetica* is a very good summary of the science he was advocating. Voegelin sought to restore the *noetic* tradition of searching for meaning and reason in the inner experience of consciousness (NSP, 2). These experiences are meant to illuminate truth and point to political reality found in our participation of the divine *nous* with the ground of being (A, 86). It intends to explore the psychopathology of alienation and the derision of reason and ultimately reveal the emptiness of the modern revolt against reason and the phenomenon of the system. This is achieved through participation, differentiation, experience-symbolization, and reason (Sandoz, 1891, 204–10). In a sense, the *Principia Noetica* is a passing of the flame of knowledge that will light our way towards order and away from untruth.

Voegelin believed that the *noetic* philosophy developed by Plato and Aristotle was the best means ever devised of participating with the divine in the conscious mind of man. *Noesis* offers a means to articulate the structure of this "inner space," and relating the knowledge derived from the exploration of this "space" to the establishment of order, law, and social morality (A, 124–30). Voegelin also studied Judeo-Christian philosophy, morality, and its effects on man's relationship to God. While Voegelin studied many religions, he concluded that Christianity provided the most differentiated experience the *noetic* philosopher could achieve. Voegelin concluded that any revised and improved *noesis* must include Judeo-Christian revelation and historiography (EA, 371–73). Ultimately, Voegelin believed that the *noetic* and revelatory experiences of spiritual participation were the defining points in history.

The *Principia Noetica* would likely be useless if it could not be applied. Application of his "science" is demonstrated in Voegelin's analysis of the German people's failure to resist Hitler in his book *Hitler and the Germans*. Voegelin critically assesses the failure of German academic, ecclesiastical, and legal segments of society to resist the moral abyss that Hitler and the National Socialists represented. There was nothing within German society to resist this movement towards immorality and sub-human existence because they had placed their faith in one man, not in the divine ground of being. As the *Principia Noetica* makes clear, God is the only thing man has to resist the "mortalizing forces of the *apeirontic* lust of being in time" (A, 113). In the rejection of the divine *nous (ratio)*, there is very little to prevent man from relenting to a darker nature that feels alienated and yearns for the bliss of not suffering within the "present" of a human life

The next section will conclude this guide. Some perspectives on Voegelin's impact, his critics, the science he proposes, and how to live the *noetic* life will be detailed.

# CONCLUSION — POLITICAL REALITY

## C.1 Eric Voegelin's Contribution to Science and Understanding

Eric Voegelin was clearly a learned and intelligent man. These are rather common characteristics for a stand-out academic. What set Voegelin apart were his imagination, vision, and relentless determination. His ability to open to the mystery that lies at the outer limits of human experiences in consciousness and resistance to the positivistic forces in his profession make him unique. These traits guided him on a long journey to restore some measure of a lost humanity that Voegelin felt had led modern man to feel alienated and suffer under dehumanizing political orders. He had to create a science based on past traditions of Western culture and envisions new ways for modernity to preserve its consciousness and ordering experiences. So, how did he do? What did he contribute? In his 2002 book *Eric Voegelin,* Michael Federici enumerates seven contributions to science and understanding (183), which I have placed in the order that seems most fitting:

1) Diagnosed the Western crisis.
2) Developed a philosophical framework of openness to the transcendent that can be used to restore order to Western civilization.
3) Recovery of the symbols and engendering experiences of order.
4) The restoration of political science via a critique of positivism.
5) A critical analysis of totalitarianism and modern ideological movements.
6) Developed a philosophy of consciousness.
7) Developed a philosophy of history.

To all of this, we can add the *Principia Noetica*, which encapsulates most of these ideas but offers a way to understand the restoration of Western transcendental experience, man's relationship to reason and spirit, and how it can be applied. He paved a way for man to think beyond modern immanentist paradigms and reminded us that the transcendental reality of our past remains valid and beneficial in the continuing pursuit of order. His resistance to those forces that sought to deny and marginalize the divine and transcendent in human experience serves as a reminder that we should never come to believe that a simple policy change or bureaucratic system can change human nature. Asserting that reality is found in the truth of our divine nature, which is the ground of our being (and this alone creates order), simply gives one pause to consider the implications of God and our relationship to Him in a social and political context. Of course, taking a position of this kind can lead to some criticism, and that will be discussed next.

## C.2 His Critics

### *Isolation and Philosophy*

Critically judging Voegelin's contribution can be as important as understanding it. Despite his creative and insightful genius, his work is not without flaws. Because Voegelin was an intellectual omnivore who consumed volumes of history, religion, philosophy, law, and works in his own field of political theory, assessing his body of work is challenging. The following is not an exhaustive list of critiques, but covers essential disagreements and weaknesses of Voegelin's work.

Voegelin remained a member of the political science community throughout his career, but he came to think of himself as a mystic philosopher and certainly did pursue philosophical interests. It is perhaps here that we can make a general criticism of Voegelin's body of work. As a political theorist, he worked most closely with individuals in his field. He was never, and perhaps by no fault of his own, seriously tested by the academic rigor of professional philosophers. His philosophic methods and determinations were those of a political scientist working on philosophical problems, who never faced the challenge of full-fledged scrutiny by those trained in the field who might have shed light on problems with his theories and methods (Walsh, 2007, 12–13). This allowed Voegelin to raise and answer philosophical questions on his own. Once he was satisfied with an answer he could leave the issue as settled and go on his way to the next concentrated focus on a new question (Walsh, 2007, 13).

Despite a rich history of correspondence with others, conference attendance, and colleagues at the universities of his employ, Voegelin worked mostly in isolation. Given the amount that he read and the volume of written words he produced, this was probably necessary. The general problem with this approach was that his work lacked the insight and oversight that collaborative work fosters. He did not enjoy the constant scrutiny of others that can be critical in refining and improving products, especially given that the topics he chose were of such enormity. Voegelin was heavily influenced by the existence of totalitarian regimes that were edging close to destroying humanity during most of his career. Perhaps because of this Voegelin's isolation and preoccupation with resisting the Gnosticism he saw everywhere in modernity could lead him to draw conclusions that were excessively influenced by fear and pessimism (Walsh, 2007, 13). Of course he did receive input from peers, mostly through correspondence and interaction with colleagues, but he was not "working" with them in the full sense of the word. The right team of collaborators could have been helpful in improving some of his conclusions and tempering his occasionally over-zealous quest of exposing modern Gnosticism. Collaboration with philosophers might have opened Voegelin up to some of the growing post-Kantian developments that were paralleling his own work (Walsh, 2007, 17).

### Symbols

David Walsh, the former chair of the Political Science Department at Catholic University of America in Washington D.C. (who also holds a Master's in Philosophy) and proponent of Voegelin's work, points out that Voegelin missed some of the philosophical implications of the "reality-experience-symbol" symbolic construct. Walsh believes this does not quite capture the dynamic character of existence in which reality is never actually present. Much like the "mystery" itself, we are always falling short of truly encountering it. We can sense it, but can we know its truth? Walsh asserts that modern philosophy is arriving at the conclusion that it is precisely our lateness of apprehension that opens the possibility of existence, as humanity exists within the unending movement toward what can never finally be reached (Walsh, 2007, 21–22). Voegelin's approach to the question of "Being" remains too closely tied to the historic aspiration of naming it (Walsh, 2007, 19). His was a transcendental conception and as such should have implied that truth in "Being" is just what cannot become present or revealed, and yet Voegelin takes the opposite tack and describes mostly what is "revealed" (Walsh, 2007, 20).

Another long-time proponent of Voegelin, John Hallowell, notes in "Existence in Tension: Man in Search of His Humanity" (1972), that Voegelin does make detailed studies of myth, philosophy, revelation, and mysticism as the means by which men may partially understand the order of "Being." However, Voegelin does not make precise distinctions among these terms, which complicates the process of differentiation and assigning symbols (Rossbach, 2005, 89) (Hallowell, 1972, 183). Furthermore, Hallowell insists this begs the question of how the average man or the *noetic* can discern the good symbols from those that reflect a deformation of reality when there isn't enough distinction between philosophy, myth, and revelation to determine an answer. Voegelin himself described the inherent difficulty in producing both illuminating symbols and objectifying type-concepts:

> The questions touch a cardinal problem inherent to the analysis of existential consciousness, the inherent temptation that is every questioner's burden, the temptation to deform the Beyond and its formative *parousia*, as they are experienced and symbolized in the respective quest, by transforming the Beyond into a thing and its *parousia* into the imposition of a definite form on reality. The temptation not only affects the present analysis, but is a constant force in the millennial process of the quest for truth (ISO, 33).

### Gnosticism

The most heavily criticized area of Voegelin's work was his use of the term Gnostic and the various ways he extrapolated its meaning. As discussed in Chapter 1, Voegelin struggled with the best articulation of all the various meanings found in the word. Although its use as a heuristic device met with general approval, the term suffered from several difficulties. There are several reasons why this term is not wholly satisfactory, and one simple fact stands out more than the others: the ancient Gnostics sought to escape the world; the modern Gnostics want to change it (Sandoz, 2006, 149). The ancient Gnostics saw nothing worth living for in this world and yearned for life in a radically transcendent cosmos, whereas the modern Gnostic sees the suffering in life and believes he can "build a better mouse trap" that will alleviate the suffering. In the *New Science of Politics,* Voegelin describes modernity as the essence of Gnosticism with man placing himself at the center of order by using science and systems to bring on a utopia and thereby replacing God at the seat of order (NSP, 133). This seems a far cry from the ancient people's desire to escape the mortal world.

According to Voegelin, Western modernity began somewhere around 1500 and runs to the present (NSP, 116). This has been an era marked by what Voegelin felt was the explosive revolt against Western civilization traditions largely founded on Christianity and Greek philosophy. The explosive revolts included the Reformation and the Enlightenment. There certainly was a revolt during this period in the sense that humanity experienced a series of personal, intellectual, and spiritual revolts against the limitations and imperfections of human existence. However, it seems unlikely that the original Gnostics and their writings were the cause of modernity's anti-theological, anti-Hellenic mass-movement proponents like Marx or Hegel (Franz, 2005, 42–43). It is more likely born of the common experience found in the *metaxy* where the experience of the "Gnostics" found a common "malformation," rather than a chain of ancient writings that directly influenced modernity (Franz, 2005, 43).

Additionally, the research on ancient Gnosticism since Voegelin's publication of the *New Science of Politics* has advanced considerably. As a result, his picture of ancient Gnostics had become outmoded. Voegelin had derived his foundational perspective of Gnosticism on Hans Jonas's *Gnosis und Spätantiker Geist*, published in 1934 (Webb, 2008, 53). Jonas had used the only texts available to research the issue, all of which came from Christian writings of the day directly or indirectly commenting about various people and societies they describe as Gnostic. Jonas admits to imaginatively filling in some blanks and self-selecting who belonged to the groups (Webb, 2008, 55). The term itself is a little confusing given its Greek origin, and the fact that it was not something any one group called itself. The term was merely a Christian intellectual label. Jonas described the Gnostics as: "an anti-cosmic nihilism that despairs of the possibility that life in this world could be good under any circumstances" (Webb, 2008, 53). At any rate, the release of "Gnostic" texts from the *Nag Hamadi* library since 1970 offered direct writings from the groups labeled Gnostic, which has completely altered the conception of them, particularly as Jonas presented (Webb, 2008, 61). This new information confirms a common theme of dualism within the groups considered to be "Gnostic"; however, the views of the groups originally listed by Jonas and accepted by Voegelin were not at all homogenous or espousing a singular message as Jonas's work imputed. For this reason Webb, Franz, Rossbach and others remained discontent on the clarity between ancient and modern Gnostics. However, Voegelin believed there was a clear thread (SPG, 9). Therefore the best means to avoid confusion is to recall that ancient Gnostics sought a transcendental escape from reality, while modern Gnostics seek to maximize human programs to change the immanent world and reject any notion of transcendental reality (Sandoz, 206, 149). The thread they share is a profound dissatisfaction with the human condition in the present, and a desire to do something about it.

As described in Chapter one, Voegelin had a long list of descriptive terms that enhanced or replaced Gnosis over the thirty-plus years after the publication of the *New Science of Politics*. Voegelin did not change his belief that modernity, and Western civilization particularly, suffered from a spiritual deformation that led to a loss of truth and a lapse into unreality (Federici, 2002, 20–21). This of course was a phenomenon to be resisted. Any movement that embraced a human order rejecting the divine ground of Being and sought an intra-mundane salvation for man through human action was the phenomenology to be identified and in some way labeled "Gnostic." The use of various terms such as "egophany," "egophanic revolt," "pneumopathology," "doxic reason," "metastasis," "resistance to reality," "deformation of existence," "refusal to apperceive," and even "schizophrenia" to describe the general concept basically called "Gnosticism" made sense given the wide applications Voegelin used for the idea over his career (Rossbach, 2005, 89). However, it made actual analysis (empirical or otherwise) of this phenomenon extremely difficult. Comprehension of the various terms becomes situational, subjective, and difficult to expand into a singular concept that has its origins in antiquity and directly influences modernity with its "modern age defining" presence of God-less mass movements. That does not mean Voegelin was not identifying a real phenomenon, just that the thirty years of alteration made his concept harder to clearly understand, and the terms he used to describe it hard to follow outside of the context in which they were used. This possibly detracted from the remarkable work he produced and made concrete philosophic testing and analysis of his ideas problematic.

### Christianity

Although not in complete agreement with him, Voegelin found widespread and often enthusiastic support for his works among Christian scholars until the publication of *Order and History: IV, The Ecumenic Age* (1975). This book brought distressed and thought-provoking responses from an array of scholars who criticized Voegelin's revised conceptions of revelation and Christianity. The criticism ranged from Voegelin underestimating the effects of Christian revelation on the structure of reality to overestimating the relationship between Christianity and modern Gnostic movements (Federici, 2002, 168). The focus on Paul as the central experience of Christianity rather than Christ and His Incarnation was nothing short of shocking to the faithful (Federici, 2002, 169). The placing of primary emphasis on Greek philosophy over Christian faith, dogma, and doctrine was seen as a tragic lack of understanding of the role of these important components to promulgating the message and meaning of Christ's crucifixion and resurrection (Federici, 2002, 169). These criticisms were far more than equivocations over Voegelin's interpretation of Christianity, and directly challenged his new-founded philosophical project. The central debate focused on whether the Christians' claim that Christ's revelation provides completeness of meaning in the unfinished process of history, or was Voegelin correct that any finality of meaning in history would be impossible for the philosopher to accept? There is no readily available resolution to this incredibly difficult question and there remain many criticisms of Voegelin's *Ecumenic Age* conclusions by Christian scholars.

### Flaws Do Not Limit Value

It is impossible to work in academia and not be criticized and Voegelin was no exception. There is a wide spectrum of critical analysis of his work that ranges from the valid to the outright ridiculous, the most frivolous being that Voegelin is impossible to understand. That's true only if you do not read the scholarly work he produced. Voegelin's work can be dense, the subject matter difficult, terminologically confusing, ever evolving, oddly inclusive and exclusive, and challenging—but it is not incomprehensible. He forces you to think, to read supporting works, to dig into history, ask deep questions, explore things on your own, and actually work hard at understanding him. This can be too much for those who want easily digestible, "cookie cutter" answers. No doubt, his work has flaws. Despite these flaws, Voegelin offers a rare chance to dig deeply into the nature of humanity and that special place of mystery and meaning that has yielded some of man's greatest knowledge. The flaws are worth noting, but should not prevent anyone from benefiting from the exploration of his incredibly important work.

## C.3 Did Voegelin Answer the Question of Political Reality?

### Answering the Question

As discussed, Voegelin made contributions to science and knowledge. He also produced brilliant yet humanly flawed philosophy. With the flaws and esoteric nature of the work, is it possible that he answered the question originally proposed in this guide? Can we say that by utilizing the exploration of consciousness found in the *Principia Noetica* we can know political reality? It seems the answer is "yes," but a qualified yes would be more precise. The reality we come to know through Voegelin is a transcendental one, which if applied properly, provides powerful insights into the nature of man, society, and politics. Certainly, recognizing these dimensions of participation in a human life creates an opening to see the structure of reality for the individual. To exploit this opening, the participant in the act of conscious exploration must reach out in the *metaxic* "In-between" and sense the spiritual substance that illuminates the truth of existence. If in this experience the participant recognizes what orders "souls" and society, then the participant will have achieved a differentiated experience of truth and can see a reality that can extend to the political. If the participant chooses symbols wisely, he can relay this knowledge in a productive way. Walking through this process again makes an obvious implication: Voegelin's new science asserts that immanent reality can only be properly interpreted through transcendental reality.

It is here that we find the qualifications for our "yes" to reality. Voegelin's is a radically transcendent method of achieving an understanding of reality. Despite the depth of content in his work it can also be abstract. That our material reality must be seen through transcendence leaves society and order hanging in the balance based on the esoteric skills of a few mystic philosophers. Human skill at plumbing the depths of our psyche will certainly yield a more insightful and circumspect participant in the material world. How adept a society's mystic practitioners are at the exploration of consciousness, understanding the experience and translating meaning, then articulating the symbols, will probably vary wildly on a given day and subject matter at hand. And yet they remain Voegelin's best hope for order.

This can be a hard concept for modernity to accept, as it seems arbitrary and vulnerable to all manner of mundane manipulation. But here Voegelin makes a blunt point: what other tool do we have to explore the reality yielding human "soul" but consciousness? When humans deal collectively with their fellows, what better tool do they have for treating others with compassion than the "soul" (*nous*)? Our "observer" mind recognizes others' existence, but is that sufficient to recognize the potential "equal-ness" in others that deserves justice on par with our own? In a sense, what Voegelin is suggesting is that if man has a soul, it is this part of his nature that recognizes the soul in other people. This recognition is a reaching out to the divine in others, in the same sense that *nous* reaches out to the divine in the *metaxy*. If we base social and political order on this notion of "spirit"-based equality (*imago dei*) and apply it universally with law (more natural than positive law), then order will move in the direction of legitimacy and stability. Voegelin only seems abstract morally and politically because what he describes philosophically is "being directed by knowing" and the knowing comes from participation with the divine.

Beyond all the discussion of philosophy, religion, and history, Voegelin reveals the complexity in acting simply and responsibly within society. It is up to the participant to know himself and see himself in others, thereby creating the bond of recognition and good will. Voegelin describes the process of knowing yourself, sharpening your tools for recognizing reality, while providing a veritable Master's course on how to remain concrete while experiencing the otherworldly reality of the psyche. With this knowledge, citizens can act in society with a deeper sense of what is real because they recognize how others should be treated *justly*. This form of thought and action should help one avoid dominating and cruel treatment of others (*libido dominandi*), as this form of treatment should be objectionable to you personally, and therefore equally objectionable to others. Because human activity covers an incredibly wide range of possibilities, the skill of differentiation becomes much more important in applying this knowledge. Recognizing the untruths that make ill treatment of others acceptable for the sake of power is to be resisted. Because there is the divine, we have a greater responsibility to act morally than we might otherwise find without divinity. Divinity also offers a way to live with imperfection and understand our limitations in attempting to move beyond and somehow transform our nature. This is a process, not a set of dogmas or policies. This is political reality.

Just as our ancestors did, Voegelin is delineating "truth" in the process of being human. Voegelin's political theory details the *process* of *metanoia* as man seeks to transform disorder to order and finds the means to do so in the experience with the sacred in consciousness. Voegelin's is a science of verbs: participation, experience, differentiation, assigning symbols, reasoning, articulating, being, knowing, recalling, questioning, judging, orienting, and sensing tension. It is being alive in this moment in the full and conscious participation with the divine to best enable an individual and his society to seek and live in order. This is not a description of systems, but the action of process. The process is historical as it defines time, personal as it requires an individual to utilize *anamnesis* and experience the divine *nous* in the *metaxy,* social in that the individual must articulate truth through symbol to his peers and they must accept it, and political as the ground of being revealed as the base of order with its hierarchy under the divine which creates the paradigm for law and government that best reflects social morality. Truth, reason, and spirit bind the society in divine-human order that is just, and the absence of any of them is the source of dissolution, dehumanization, ignorance, and disorder—in short, the way of Gnosis. This is the ultimate illumination of human political reality. The Western crisis is the loss of this once traditional view of humanity, reality, and way to a more perfect order.

It is this quality of action that makes Voegelin's science so revolutionary. Simply understanding is not enough. One must *act* to know anything. It is a call to spiritual and intellectual arms where great things are possible if we are willing to work hard to get them. In a sense, this is a natural human process, and one that man has participated in throughout human existence. But it is fragile and easily lost because, like the home fires of old, it must be constantly tended or it will die out. Voegelin sparks the metaphorical flame and passes the torch of the ancient fire of knowledge and spirit. It is not up to him to decide the best symbols for divine order; it is up to every individual to either use *noesis* to discover it for himself or believe in those who offer truth found in the experience. It is society's sacred responsibility to follow this truth toward order through just and moral treatment in social and political activity. Voegelin's flame is the light in Plato's cave that does not cast shadows, but instead lights the way beyond the cave.

### *Living* La Vida Noetica

The process of participation does require some guideposts along the way. In *Anamnesis*, Voegelin provides a means to learn how the process unfolds and what to expect along the way. In effect, *Anamnesis* offers instructions for living *la vida Noetica* to the political scientist and citizen alike. To live in accordance with Voegelin's philosophic conceptions, the *noetic* practitioner would need to cultivate certain directed, meditative skills. The process of recalling "aha" moments is useful in both sharpening meditative skills and generating the "spirit" necessary to move into the *metaxy*. Learning to orient in the "In-Between" would require the habit of repeated experiences in higher and directed meditation to both understand the experience and differentiate the meaning of the experience. Both the relenting to and sharpening of the skill of questioning the "mystery" while having a *metaxic* experience, yields higher-quality differentiated knowledge. Apperception and study of the experience would yield the best symbols, and recognition of the spiritual state of society would assist in offering the best articulation of the symbols.

This is a contemplative life in the mode of the *bios theoretikos*. Beyond exploration of the metaxy, it requires acting in a manner that is *just* toward fellow citizens, and taking responsibility for yourself and society. Self-reflection and apperception are daily practices and the study of humanity, politics, philosophy, society, and religion your vocation. There are six general principles to follow:

1) Use *anamnesis* and *noesis* to achieve *metanoia*
2) Understand the founding ideas and symbols of your nation's political ideals
3) Analyze the general state of society and relation to political order
4) Investigate possibility of a "second ordered reality"
5) Apply common sense
6) Resist social and political calls to place order outside the ground of being

### Scientific Application of Principia Noetica to Diagnose Political Reality

As demonstrated in *Hitler and the Germans*, Voegelin's *Principia Noetic* can be used in practical analysis of real-world political problems. Any political theorist of our day could apply Voegelin's *Principia Noetica* in analyzing a particular society and likely determine the level of vulnerability to Gnostic forces the society is currently experiencing. For the political scientist well versed in *Principia*, the investigation can begin by looking to see if the science honored in the observed society is highly restricted to the natural sciences and whether science values philosophical explorations of human truth. Through the application of reason, and with knowledge of the spirit, the political scientist can examine any given society and determine if the psychopathology of alienation from the divine is occurring by determining the extent to which the ground of being is accepted as the basis of order. An investigation of the relationship between the spiritual institutions and society should be looking for signs of an exclusionary religious dogma and the sanction of discriminatory legal practices for those outside the sacraments.

The investigation should then turn to a review of the state legal and governmental institutions. Within the state, the theorist's examination will require looking for the dilution of individual rights, a state that promises liberation through mass movement that culminates in a utopia, seeks to use propaganda and other measures to create a second ordered reality, places excessive control over the legal system in the hands of a single branch of government, allows expansive civil rights for one group within society but severely restricts another, and exercises dehumanizing and brutal physical and psychological control measures over the citizenry. If you find all of these scientific, social, religious, and governmental malformations, then you will have found a society in the grips of a full Gnostic revolt, and human suffering on a grand scale close at hand. Graduated scales of disorder could be created to determine the extent of the problem. This is one possible application of Voegelin's *noetic* science in discovering and diagnosing political reality.

The use of *anamnesis* and development of abilities in consciousness to enter the *metaxy* and know reason and spirit of the divine *nous (ratio)* makes diagnosing ideological and Gnostic movements possible with a greater degree of insight and accuracy. With *metaxic* knowledge the rejection of a man-made utopia will be a simple matter of common sense. This is the science of Plato and Aristotle and facilitates participation and differentiation in the constant process of defining reality through conscious participation in the *metaxy*. In the process of being, the *noetic* scientist should live in the knowledge that life is a gift and we honor the sacred when we respect it as Plato and St. Paul taught. The symbols that best capture this process are "consciousness-reality-language" and "intentionality-luminosity-reflective distance" (ISO, 13–18). "Results" must always be accompanied with the considerations that produced them and equivalent symbols will be just as effective at both understanding order and diagnosing the current state of spiritual health of a society. This is a living and continuous process with marked open exploration of an experiential and present reality.

## C.4 A Few Closing Thoughts on What Eric Voegelin Taught Us

Eric Voegelin was regarded as one of the great political thinkers of the twentieth century (Sandoz, 1981, 8). However, his political theory and name are not as well known as other theorists like Max Weber, Hannah Arendt, or Leo Strauss. There are a number of possible reasons for this, but the most likely are the complexity of his works, the sheer volume of the required reading, and the lack of a simple way to sum up his work. Voegelin does not believe in having a dogmatic, systematic, or simple set of rules for adherents to follow (Federici, 2002, 187). If there were a metaphoric shape that defines his theories, it would be a fog bank. The observer can see it, but it is hard to see through, constantly changing shape, and has thicker and thinner segments. But it is not impenetrable, just difficult to navigate. It takes time and effort to read through his work, and then even more time to try out his *anamnestic* techniques, explore the ancient Greek philosophers, construct a dictionary of terms, read about the prophets of revelation, come to grips with historiography, and read through his critiques of Gnostic Enlightenment thinkers. Reading and thinking are required. It is an investment of time that most political scientists are unwilling to make, but if one does, he will be richly rewarded.

We have grown accustomed to science offering set systems to both identify and correct political problems. Voegelin never advocates for a particular governmental formation; instead he uses an approach reminiscent of the *via negativa* to explain what does not work (Sandoz, 1981, 201–2). The *polis* offers no sanctuary for modern man given its restrictive size. Authoritarianism works in certain situations but is undesirable given its disregard for the rights of the individual. Communism and National Socialism are dreadful ideologies and an abomination to mankind. Ancient Rome worked on certain levels, when the church and state were one, but when those functions split, it became less stable. It too suffered from a lack of humanity. However, the constitutional liberal democracies of the Anglo-sphere offer some hope. For Voegelin the United States and United Kingdom presented the very best resistance to the revolutionary communist and Nazi movements, both physically and spiritually (A, 213). Western democracies promote God, individual rights, separation of powers, clear symbols with which to base their constitutions, and other economic and legal benefits (Federici, 2002, 15–16, 18). However, Voegelin also saw trouble ahead for liberal democracies in general. He took the near worship of material well-being and attempted cordoning-off of religious beliefs into a purely private sphere as symptoms of the spiritual crisis unfolding in the Western democracies (Federici, 2002, 17).

In Voegelin's estimation, Britain and the United States had seen less destruction of the Western classical and Christian cultural foundations than other European countries (A, 213). Because of this, he felt the British and American societies had retained more cultural resources with which to combat the growing disorder present in Europe (NSP, 189). Part of his desire to return to Germany in 1958 was prompted by the hope of promoting an American-inspired political system in his native land (AR, 91). He did not, however, devote volumes of work to advocating or examining democracy like so many of his contemporaries. This was a point of some criticism for those who felt Voegelin had not given enough credit to liberal constitutions and democracy (Federici, 2002, 186). Perhaps this is a fair assessment; however, Voegelin was more intent on capturing the traditions he felt more closely aligned social and political order and left analysis on the modes of government to others (Federici, 2002, 186). From this perspective, it is easier to understand that instead of prescribing a single system for all people in all times, Voegelin saw the need for a people, in their time and circumstance, to define on their own the best political system to promote truth, reason, and equal protection for all under the *imago Dei* (Federici, 2002, 64, 190) (HG, 204–5). He emphasized the process of choosing how best to ensure order over the final form it took (Federici, 2002, 64).

Voegelin recognized there were a number of governmental configurations that could achieve order. He did come to the conclusion that, despite the many flaws of liberal-style democracy, it is best suited to nurture the essentials for order at present (Federici, 2002, 64–65). But be warned: if a given society chooses a democracy, certain traits of the people must be instilled or folly and human suffering will occur on a grand scale (Federici, 2002, 65).

Taking Voegelin's work as a whole, a recipe for maintaining order within a society makes itself known. The society must find ways to cultivate men and women capable of either seeking the truth of the divine *nous*, or are wise enough to listen to those that do. Those inclined to enter the *metaxy* must have the ability to spiritually orient and to act with both reason and spirit in daily life. They must be literate enough to articulate truth and reality. Leadership is more difficult in democracy and requires citizens who are endowed with human authority, which includes those who can lead and those who can follow such authority. All of this must come to pass while resisting the siren call of the "rabble." Each citizen must recognize that he is subject to God's law, which both endows him with protections and requires that he recognize the judgment under which he lives. Each citizen is obliged to judge himself and his neighbor and make decisions that are *just* for both. This judgment extends to the elected and unelected representatives of society. If the representatives act unjustly, foolishly, illegally, or capriciously, the citizens are responsible and must take action to resolve the negative outcomes of these acts and find better representatives. Even in the best of circumstances, this will be difficult to both develop and maintain and will require a consistent state of literacy. There will be an ebb and flow in adherence to these principles and understanding of them, but with a base of reason and spirit, it can be done. It is probably best to let Eric Voegelin summarize this point with the last word:

"… the spiritual disorder of our time, the civilizational crisis of which everyone so readily speaks, does not by any means have to be borne as an inevitable fate; that, on the contrary, everyone possesses the means of overcoming it in his own life. And our effort should not only indicate the means, but also how to employ them. No one is obliged to take part in the spiritual crises of society; on the contrary, everyone is obliged to avoid the folly and live his life in order" (CW, Vol. 5, 261).

# REFERENCES

Federici, Michael. 2002. *Eric Voegelin*. Wilmington, DE. Intercollegiate Studies Institute.

Franz, Michael. 2005. The Concept of Gnosticism and the Analysis of Spiritual Disorder. *Political Science Reviewer*. Vol. 34: 28–47.

Germino, Dante. 1978. Eric Voegelin's Framework for Political Evaluation in His Recently Published Work. *The American Political Science Review* Vol. 72, No. 1: 110–21.

Geoffrey L. Price. 1994. Eric Voegelin: A Classified Bibliography. Bulletin of the John Rylands University Library of Manchester, vol. 76, No. 2 (Summer).

Marx, Karl. 1845. *Theses on Feuerbach (11)*. Translated by Cyril Smith 2002. In the Karl Marx Digital Library, http://www.marxists.org/archive/marx/works/1845/theses/

Rossbach, Michael. 2005. "Gnosis" in Eric Voegelin's Philosophy. *Political Science Reviewer* Vol. 34: 77.

Sandoz, Ellis. 1981. *The Voegelin Revolution*. Baton Rouge, LA: Louisiana State University Press.

Sandoz, Ellis. 2006. *Republicanism, Religion, and the Soul of America*. Columbia, MO: University of Missouri Press.

Sandoz, Ellis. 2009. "The Philosopher's Vocation: The Voegelinian Paradigm," *Review of Politics* Vol. 71: 54–67.

Sandoz, Ellis. 2013. *Give Me Liberty*. South Bend, IN. St. Augustine Press.

Voegelin, Eric. 1952. *The New Science of Politics*. Chicago: University of Chicago Press.

Voegelin, Eric. 1968. *Science, Politics and Gnosticism*. Wilmington, DE. Intercollegiate Studies Institute.

Voegelin, Eric. 1975. *From Enlightenment to Revolution*. Durham, NC. Duke University Press.

Voegelin, Eric. 1978. *Anamnesis*. Notre Dame: Notre Dame University Press.

Voegelin, Eric. 1989. *Autobiographical Reflections*. Baton Rouge, LA: Louisiana State University Press.

Voegelin, Eric. 1990. "Response to Professor Altizer's A New History and a New but Ancient God?" in Voegelin, *The Collected Works of Eric Voegelin. Published Essays, 1966–1985. Vol. 12.* Columbia, MO: University of Missouri Press. 293–94.

Voegelin, Eric. 1999. *Hitler and the Germans*. Columbia, MO: University of Missouri Press.

Voegelin, Eric. 2000. *The Collected Works of Eric Voegelin. The Ecumenic Age, Order and History Vol. IV*. Columbia, MO: University of Missouri Press.

Voegelin, Eric. 2000. *The Collected Works of Eric Voegelin. In Search of Order, Order and History Vol. V*. Columbia, MO: University of Missouri Press.

Voegelin, Eric. 2000. *The Collected Works of Eric Voegelin. The Theory of Governance and Other Miscellaneous Papers 1921–1938*. Columbia, MO: University of Missouri Press.

Voegelin, Eric. 2001. *The Collected Works of Eric Voegelin. Israel and Revelation, Order and History Vol. 1*. Columbia, MO: University of Missouri Press.

Voegelin, Eric. 1984. "The Meditative Origin of the Philosophical Knowledge of Order," (transl. by Frederick Lawrence), in Fred Lawrence (ed.). *The Beginning and the Beyond: Papers from, the Gadamer and Voegelin Conferences*, Supplementary Issue of the Lonergan Workshop Vol.4. Chico, CA: Scholars Press: 47–48.

Walsh, David. 2007. Voegelin's Place in Modern Philosophy. *Modern Age* 49, Issue 1 (Winter): 12–23.

Webb, Eugene. 2005. Voegelin's "Gnosticism" Reconsidered. *Political Science Reviewer,* Vol. 34: 48–76.

# VITA

Colonel Montgomery C. Erfourth, United States Army, gradu- ated from the University of Florida in 1993 with a Bachelor of Arts degree in political Science. He was commissioned a Second Lieutenant in the United States Marine Corps that same year. He served sixteen years in the Marine Corps before transferring to the United States Army as a Lieutenant Colonel to take a position as a Strategic Planner. The Army allowed him a sabbatical to earn a Master of Arts in political science from Louisiana State University and he graduated in December 2013. Colonel Erfourth served in Iraq, across the Middle East and Asia, and with several Special Operations Commands the remaining five years of his 27-year military career.

His interests include ancient Greek philosophy, the history of political thought, and seeking ways to apply more complex analysis to political-military planning. While at Special Operations Command, he authored several papers on strategic design, Special Forces support to grand strategy, and lead the development for the Campaign Plan – Global Special Operations.

# INDEX